© 2008 Laurie Coulter (text)
© 2008 Martha Newbigging (illustrations)
Edited by Barbara Pulling
Designed by Sheryl Shapiro

Annick Press Ltd.

We acknowledge the support of the Canada Council for the Arts, the Ontario Arts Council, and the Government of Canada through the Book Publishing Industry Development Program (BPIDP) for our publishing activities.

Cataloging in Publication

Coulter, Laurie, 1951 -
      Ballplayers and bonesetters : one hundred ancient Aztec and Maya jobs you might have adored or abhorred / by Laurie Coulter ; art by Martha Newbigging.

Includes index.
Target audience: For ages 9-12.
ISBN 978-1-55451-141-9 (bound).—ISBN 978-1-55451-140-2 (pbk.)

      1. Aztecs—Employment—Juvenile literature. 2. Mayas—Employment—Juvenile literature. 3. Indians of Central America—Employment—Juvenile literature. 4. Occupations—Central America—History—Juvenile literature. 5. Aztecs—Juvenile literature. 6. Mayas—Juvenile literature. 7. Indians of Central America—Juvenile literature.
I. Newbigging, Martha II. Title.

HD8068.C69 2008   j331.700972'09024   C2008-902132-0

ributed in Canada by:
Books Ltd.
ek Crescent
ond Hill, ON
H1

d in the U.S.A. by Annick Press (U.S.) Ltd.
d in the U.S.A. by:
oks (U.S.) Inc.
38
ion
14205

na.

ww.annickpress.com
oulter at: www.lauriecoulter.net
Newbigging at: www3.sympatico.ca/martha.newbigging

BALLPLAYERS AND BONESETTERS

One Hundred Ancient Aztec and Maya Jobs You Might Have Adored or Abhorred

by Laurie Coulter
art by Martha Newbigging

annick press

toronto + new york + vancouv

Dis
Firef
66 L
Richm
L4B 1

Publishe
Distribut
Firefly Bo
P.O. Box 1
Ellicott Sta
Buffalo, NY

Printed in Ch

Visit us at: w
Visit Laurie C
Visit Martha

To Mark and Alyssa
—L.C.

To Owen and Simon
—M.N.

Contents

Introduction

"**M**eso" means "middle," so Mesoamerica means Middle America. Today we use the term "Middle America" to describe ordinary people living in the United States. But there was nothing ordinary about the Aztecs, Maya, and other ancient Mesoamericans. Even where they lived is extraordinary—a region of sandy seacoasts, tropical rainforest lowlands, and dry highland basins surrounded by towering volcanoes. Is it any wonder that Mesoamerica was one of only six areas on the planet where civilizations popped up all on their own?

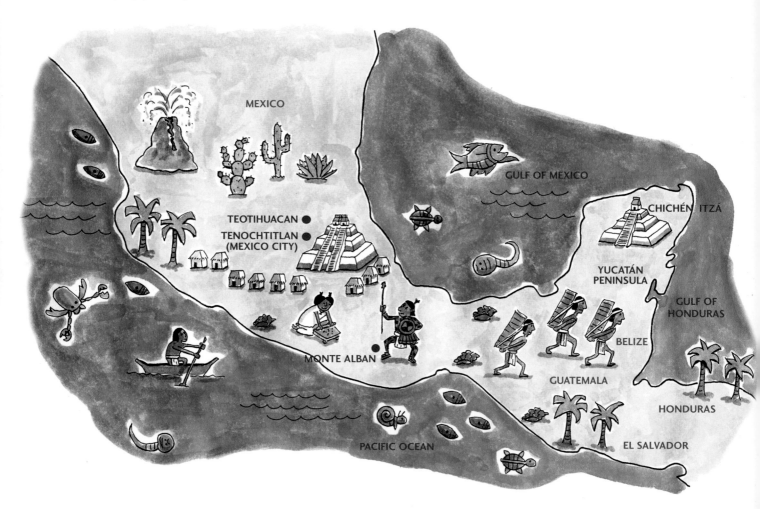

MEXICO

GULF OF MEXICO

CHICHÉN ITZÁ

TEOTIHUACAN ●
TENOCHTITLAN ●
(MEXICO CITY)

YUCATÁN
PENINSULA

GULF OF
HONDURAS

MONTE ALBAN ●

BELIZE

GUATEMALA

HONDURAS

PACIFIC OCEAN

EL SALVADOR

You can't just decide one day that you're going to be "civilized." (Unless, of course, your parents have had enough of your "uncivilized" behavior and are giving you an hour to think about it.) It takes an extremely long time for people to build cities, produce enough food to feed everybody, put snobby kings and nobles in charge of them, trade goods and ideas with other groups of people, and figure out how to run governments, armies, and schools. It's a big job, and the Mesoamericans did it very well.

Mesoamerican Firsts

In our civilization, we seem to think that being first is important, so here is a list of Mesoamerican firsts and five-star-rated accomplishments to impress you:

- Mesoamericans were the first to domesticate maize (corn). They turned a wild grass into an edible vegetable, one of the most important foods in our diet today. Chocolate lovers should also thank them. They were the first to make cocoa from cacao beans.
- Like the ancient people of Egypt and the Sudan, the Mesoamericans were great pyramid builders, although their pyramids had flat tops instead of pointy ones.
- Mesoamericans invented their own writing system. Few other ancient civilizations did this. Most borrowed bits and pieces from systems that already existed.
- Mesoamericans came up with the idea of zero, an achievement shared only by the ancient civilization of northern India and Pakistan.

- Mesoamerican calendars were more accurate than the calendars of any other civilization in the world and remained so until the telescope was used to study the stars in the early 1600s.
- Mesoamericans were expert botanists and herbalists, with a wide knowledge of the healing properties of plants. Their ability to treat wounds and set broken bones was equally impressive.
- Aztec emperor Motecuhzoma II's magnificent royal palace, which covered 2.4 hectares (6 acres), was built 150 years before King Louis XIV of France built Versailles. It may be the largest state residence ever built in the Americas.
- Mesoamericans were the first people to make rubber balls and among the first to play team sports.

These accomplished people were made up of many different cultural groups, who, like people today, moved from place to place in search of a better life. This search began when the truly ancient ancestors of the Mesoamericans began traveling from Asia to the west coast of North America at the end of the last Ice Age. They made their way south. Slowly. Eventually, they settled down, started to grow food and make things, and did a lot of thinking. (Imagine not just learning to read and write, but inventing those things in the first place!) Today, the cultural area where all these amazing things happened is the southern half of Mexico, Belize, Guatemala, and neighboring parts of Honduras and El Salvador.

Learning about ancient peoples involves a great deal of guesswork. Archeologists study ruins and artifacts to find out what they can about a culture's architecture, art, and way of life. Ethnologists look at the way today's native people do certain tasks, such as tapping rubber trees, and try to figure out how their ancestors did the same jobs. This book focuses on the work people did in what archeologists call the Late Postclassic period in Mesoamerica, from 1350 to 1521 CE.

Of all the Postclassic peoples, most is known about the Aztecs, which is why they dominate this book in the same way they dominated their world. Their empire was built by the Triple Alliance, made up of the Mexica people (based at the imperial city of Tenochtitlan), the Acolhua people (based at Texcoco), and the Tepaneca people of Tlacopan.

When the Spanish explorer Hernán Cortés marched into Tenochtitlan in 1519 with his army, he overcame the Aztecs with help from other Meso-americans who were tired of being under Aztec rule. After the conquest, the Christian invaders destroyed almost all of the native people's "pagan" books. The few that remain, however, give us a taste of the remarkable cultures that thrived in this part of the world in the Postclassic period. We can also hear these people's voices through the books of Spaniards who worked and lived among them. One of these was Spanish friar Bernardino de Sahagún. He inter-viewed Aztec elders about their culture and wrote 12 books, called the *Florentine Codex*, on everything from plants and animals to rituals and proverbs.

How Do You Say "Quetzalcoatl"?

Here is how to pronounce the Nahuatl words in *Ballplayers and Bonesetters*. Once you break the longish words down into syllables, you will be pronouncing them like an Aztec in no time. For example, the god Quetzalcoatl's name is pronounced Ket-sahl-KO-ahtl; the Aztecs' name for themselves, Mexica, is pronounced Me-SHEE-kah and their capital city, Tenochtitlan, Teh-notch-TEE-tlan. To hear Nahuatl words spoken, you can visit the Mexicolore website at www.mexicolore.co.uk and search under Aztec Pages: Aztec Pronunciation.

Vowels:

a	as in "father"
ai, ay	as "I"
e	as in "red"
ey	as in "bay"
i	as in "beep"
o	as in "hope"
u	as in "rule"

Consonants:

c (followed by "a" or "o")	as in "cape"
c (followed by "e" or "i")	as in "ceremony"
c (followed by "u")	as in "quill"
h	as in "historic"
hu	as in "wait"
ll	as in "bell"
qu (followed by "a" or "o")	as in "quake"
qu (followed by "e" or "i")	as in "kite"
tl	as in "title"
x	as in "shift"
z	as in "see"

Who Was Who in Mesoamerica

The Olmecs were the first civilization to emerge in Mexico. They lived along the tropical shores of the Gulf of Mexico. During the Middle Preclassic period, they built ceremonial centers with small pyramid-temples, invented a simple writing system, and carved spectacular stone heads, some over 3 m (9 feet) high.

By 900 the people who lived in most of the great Classic Mesoamerican centers had moved away, perhaps because of climate change, crop failures, or war. During the Postclassic period that followed, populations began to grow at a fast rate. Farmers came up with ways to grow more food for more people, and ideas and goods were traded widely.

1200 BCE – 200 CE	900
	200 – 900 CE

Royal capital cities sprang up during the Classic period. The people of the Zapotec city of Monte Alban built theirs on a mountaintop in today's Mexican state of Oaxaca. On the edge of the Central Valley of Mexico, Teotihuacan, one of the largest cities of the ancient world, boasted a population of about 150,000. Its giant Pyramid of the Sun may have kept 10,000 workers busy for 20 years.

For 650 years during the Classic period, the Maya built pyramid-temples, ballcourts, and palaces, invented a complex writing system and calendars, and created paintings, sculpture, and pottery. The earliest histories of a pre-conquest society appeared in the beautiful books of the Mixtecs.

During the Early Post-classic period, coastal trade grew, and South American metalmaking skills spread to western Mexico. In central Mexico the Toltec civilization built the city of Tula, and the Maya city of Chichén Itzá rose on the Yucatán Peninsula.

The years before the Spanish Conquest are called the Late Postclassic period. The Aztec Empire expanded by conquering several hundred city-states. At its peak, the empire controlled nearly half of Mesoamerica's 1,500 kingdoms. The Tarascan king ruled over the region's second-largest empire in the west-central highlands of Mexico, while the Inca Empire conquered most of western South America.

In 1502, some Maya traders in a dugout canoe encountered Spaniards for the first time when Christopher Columbus sailed into the Gulf of Honduras. The European invasion had begun.

950 – 1150		1350 – 1521
	1150 – 1350	

Towards the end of the Middle Postclassic period, the Aztecs founded Tenochtitlan. Elsewhere in the world: Marco Polo traveled to China from 1271 to 1295, Christian crusaders tried to recapture the Holy Land from the Muslim Turks, and the Plague killed millions of people in Europe.

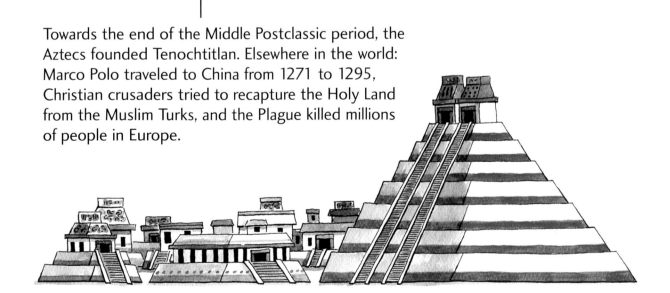

Society's Pyramid

Mesoamerican societies were divided into two classes: the nobles and the commoners. Although only about five out of every hundred men and women belonged to the elite class, those five bossed everyone else around. The best-dressed man, with the job at the top of the pyramid, was the king. Not all kings were equal, though. Some controlled empires; others made do with small city-states, or kingdoms.

Similarly, some nobles were more powerful than others. A lord's lineage (his family's ancestors) made a big difference to where he stood on the social pyramid. Some people today like to brag that they are descended from the Duke and Duchess of Some-Place-the-Rest-of-Us-Have-Never-Heard-of. Mesoamerican nobles were no different. They moved up the social ladder by marrying into families with a better genealogy chart, a larger stone house, and more luxurious clothing and jewelry. But if you think noble men and women sat around drinking cocoa all day, you are mistaken. They worked as high priests or priestesses, military officers, teachers, scribes, judges, government officials, and ambassadors.

The other 95 percent of the population formed the large base of the pyramid. They included merchants, craftspeople, farmers, and, at the very bottom, slaves. Most commoners lived in one-room adobe (sun-dried clay and straw) brick houses topped with thatched roofs. Up to five of these small houses were sometimes built by related family members around an open courtyard. Commoners had to pay the king and nobles tribute, or taxes, in the form of food, cloth, firewood, and other items. When asked, the men also had to serve as soldiers or work as laborers building temples, palaces, and canals.

Craftspeople were divided into luxury craftspeople and everyday craftspeople. The first group made jewelry, richly decorated clothes, and other luxury items for nobles. The second group made items that were used in daily life—cooking pots, knives, baskets, and plain clothes. Farmers and their wives sometimes worked part-time producing these everyday goods.

Slaves included foreigners captured in wars, commoners who were thieves or unsuccessful gamblers, and children sold into slavery by their families due to hardship. Children of slaves, though, were free as adults to work as domestic servants, overseers, or in other jobs.

Commoners could improve their social position in two ways. They could train for the priesthood, although the highest ranks were open only to nobles. Men could also gain prestige and a fancy uniform by becoming successful warriors.

During the Late Postclassic period, with populations growing and trade expanding, merchants and luxury craftspeople did very well for themselves. But they had to be careful: they couldn't display their new wealth without permission. In Mesoamerican society, the clothes and jewelry you wore told everyone where you stood on society's pyramid, what your job was, and whether you were successful at it. Poor men wore simple white maguey-fiber loincloths; noblemen dressed in decorated cotton loincloths, as well as long, colorfully patterned capes. Women in both classes wore skirts and blouses, but the noblewomen's were richly embroidered cotton rather than maguey cloth. In some cultures, commoners were forbidden to wear jewelry; in others, they couldn't wear clothes made of cotton. Only the nobles could dress like nobles.

Borrowers and Transformers

Today manufacturers make toy cars that turn into warrior robots. On television we watch fashion makeovers, house makeovers, and body makeovers—all ways that we transform ourselves and our surroundings. We wear uniforms to show others that we are nurses, soldiers, firefighters, or police officers. We look to the past for inspiration and to foreign countries for products, workers, and ideas. And some of us embrace religious beliefs to explain the unexplainable.

The Aztecs would have understood us. Their ancestors, poor hunter-gatherers from the northwest, moved into the Basin of Mexico in the mid-thirteenth century. With the people who already lived there, the Aztecs transformed themselves into empire builders in just 200 years. They ruled from Tenochtitlan, a magnificent city built on a cluster of islands in Lake Texcoco. Unlike many other empires, the Aztecs allowed the conquered city-states under their power to keep their own kings—as long as they sent regular tribute payments of food, cloth, or other goods to the Aztec emperor.

Just as your great-great-grandparents might have lived in houses with fake ancient Greek columns, or your grandparents might have collected nineteenth-century Victorian furniture, or your parents may like the "vintage" look of the 1950s, the Aztecs borrowed from two ancient cities they admired. Teotihuacan was one of the largest cities in the world until it was mysteriously abandoned by its people in the eighth century. For centuries, its ceremonial center of giant pyramids, mural-covered temples, and grand avenues lay in ruins. When the Aztecs stumbled upon it, they thought Teotihuacan was the birthplace of the gods. They borrowed what they found carved into its monuments for their own world view—a feathered serpent god they called Quetzalcoatl and a big-eyed rain god they called Tlaloc. They also copied the layout and pyramids of this once-great city to use in their own soon-to-be-great city.

Tula had been the next powerful city to spring up after Teotihuacan, but it too was deserted by its people, in this case the Toltec, by the late twelfth century. The Aztecs believed a Toltec divine ruler, whom they called Topiltzin Quetzalcoatl, had invented writing, the calendar, and all the arts and crafts. Because the Aztecs and other Mesoamerican rulers used their family histories to justify their position at the top of the social pyramid, they claimed this Toltec king as their ancestor.

Trade is a way to transform a product you have and don't need into another one you want but don't have. Each Mesoamerican kingdom became famous for trading certain items—the Tarascans for their metalwork, the Mixtecs for their goldsmithing, the Huastecs for their shellwork and black-on-white ceramics, the Maya for their cacao beans and exotic feathers from rainforest birds. As the Aztec Empire expanded, Aztec merchants traded as far south as Guatemala and perhaps as far north as New Mexico in what is now the United States. Even war didn't stop the traders, who were allowed to conduct business in safe trade zones.

A Very Crowded Cosmos

The Aztecs and other Mesoamericans were deeply religious people. Their work, as well as their private lives, was guided by their beliefs. The Mesoamerican view of the cosmos took its cue from nature. When people saw plants die and then return to life each spring, they took it as a sign that a person's life force was also indestructible. After death, the person would continue to walk in "the beyond." In the Mesoamerican cosmos, the earth stood at the center of the universe, with a nine- or thirteen-layered heaven above and a nine-layered underworld below. Several hundred deities controlled all of nature and the activities and fates of humans. During the Postclassic period, all Mesoamericans held this common world view and performed certain rituals and ceremonies to please the gods and keep the world in balance.

One of their most sacred rituals is difficult for us to understand today. Ritual human sacrifice had been practiced in ancient Mesoamerica for a long time, but became more common during the Postclassic period. Mesoamericans believed that humans and gods depended upon one another for survival. Gods and goddesses gave people the gifts of life, good health, and food. In return, humans made offerings to the gods, particularly the precious gift of human blood. Sacrificial victims included slaves and warriors captured in battle. Once the gods were fed, the sun would rise, the rains would fall, and the crops would grow.

Early Job Training

"On earth we live, we travel along a mountain peak. Over here there is an abyss, over there is an abyss. If you go over here, or if you go over there, you will fall in. You should go only in the middle, you should live only in the middle." That's what the Aztec elders said. If they lived today, they might have added, "No hanging out or doing your own thing. The gods have created an ordered world, and humans need to cooperate and work hard to keep it that way. Some people are made to rule and others to serve. Get used to it."

Children were trained from day one to fit into their place in society. Bathing and naming ceremonies were held for Aztec children at birth. A boy was given a little bow, four arrows, and a small shield. A girl was given spinning equipment. These items symbolized their future roles as warriors and spinners of yarn. Both noble and commoner children were expected to follow this path.

From the age of four, children performed certain duties at home—carrying firewood and water for the boys, spinning and sweeping for the girls. Although some noble girls were trained as priestesses, most girls were taught by their mothers at home to cook, perform household tasks, and produce crafts. By age 15, if not earlier, noble boys attended a *calmecac* attached to a temple. At this school they learned writing, history, songs, the law, astronomy, and the calendar systems, as well as how to be a courageous warrior. Especially promising commoner boys were also allowed to attend the *calmecac*. Most, however, were trained by their fathers in the family line of work and then sent to the *telpochcalli* of their district for warrior training.

Let's pretend that you are a Mesoamerican girl or boy who is ready to choose a career. Which one would you pick? There are 100 jobs in this book that will set your life spinning, spying, stone slinging, surveying, or selling—and those are just the ones beginning with *S*. All set?

Turn the page!

CHAPTER 1

City-State Jobs

According to an Aztec legend, the god Huitzilopochtli appeared before a priest and told him his people's new home would be where a great eagle sat on a prickly pear cactus. The Aztecs found the spot and began building the city of Tenochtitlan in 1325 CE. Today the eagle and the cactus appear on Mexico's flag.

With a population of about 200,000, Tenochtitlan was one of the largest cities in the world at the time of the Spanish Conquest. Seville, Spain, had 60,000 people and London, England, 50,000. Paris, France, boasted 300,000. The Aztec imperial capital on Lake Texcoco, with its colorfully decorated buildings and numerous canals, all surrounded by floating agricultural fields called *chinampas*, amazed the Spanish conquistadors. A massive pyramid-temple towered over the center of the city. It stood in a walled sacred zone that contained the priests' residences, schools, and other smaller temples. The impressive royal palace and government offices stretched beyond the religious district, followed by the two-story houses of the nobility, then the simple houses and workshops of the commoners. Today the remains of Tenochtitlan lie beneath modern-day Mexico City.

Throughout Mesoamerica, small cities or towns served as the capitals of city-states, each ruled by a king. A rectangular public plaza stood at the center of each city. The king's palace, a pyramid-temple, other public buildings, and possibly a ballcourt were built along the plaza's four sides. Farmers from the surrounding rural areas walked to town to go to the market, attend religious festivals, and pay their taxes.

Surveyor

It's your job to decide where Tenochtitlan's streets will go. The streets are more like walkways, since there aren't any wheeled vehicles or horses in Mesoamerica at this time. Four major avenues (ideal for parades) reach out north, south, east, and west from the center of the city, dividing it into quarters. The other streets run in straight lines as well—no winding streets or crescents. In ancient civilizations, only strong kings were able to plan ahead, set rules for where people would live and work, and organize a city in this way.

Outside the city, you measure farmers' fields by multiplying the width of the field by its length to find out the area. You are much more precise in your measurements than the Spaniards who take over the Aztec Empire. Your measurements are recorded on a map, along with the tax owed by the landowner.

Calpulli Governor

City-states are divided into wards, or neighborhoods, called *calpulli*. Each one has its own plots of land to be farmed by its members, who are usually related and work in the same occupation. You have been elected by members of your *calpulli* to be their *calpullec*. This full-time job is given only to a trusted elder of the community. You are in charge of keeping the maps of your ward's lands and the people who own them up to date. If a landowner dies, you rub out his name and add the new owner's. You work with the *calpulli* council to distribute vacant land, to collect tribute, and to set up temples and schools. Another elder, appointed by the king, acts as military commander of the ward's men when they go to war.

Judge

You studied Aztec law at the local *calmecac.* Judges are described as those "who listen and speak well; who are of good memory" and "who arise early." You had better be an early bird. The lower court for commoners begins at daybreak. Witnesses are called and swear upon the earth goddess to tell the truth by placing a finger in the dirt and then putting the finger on their tongue. ("To swear" in Nahuatl is *tlal-qua,* "to eat earth.") After hearing a few cases in the morning, you eat a meal brought from the royal palace, take a short break, and then return to the court. Court ends two hours before the sun sets.

Scribes (writers) make a record of the judgment in each case.

If you are a member of the higher court for nobles, your verdicts are passed along to the king, who makes the final judgment. A person who is found guilty is punished immediately. He or she is usually put to death or placed in slavery rather than locked up in a prison. The king pays you in goods every 80 days, plus you have lands and tenants to support your family. Be happy with your pay. If you accept even a small gift as a bribe, your fellow judges will chew you out. If you keep it up, your head will be shaved and you will lose your job.

Tribute Collector

Don't expect people to be happy to see you in this job. Nobody likes the tax collector. You collect taxes once, twice, or four times a year. Landholding commoners pay tribute based on the size and quality of their land. A hilly field is not taxed as highly as a flat one. Taxpayers may hand you 20 cacao beans or a pile of firewood or a few turkeys. If you're tempted to lie about what is owed and demand four birds instead of two, so that you can keep two for yourself, you might want to know the penalty: death.

Latrine Boatman

"I must also mention, with all apologies, that they sold many canoe-loads of human excrement," wrote a Spanish soldier in 1519. Hey, is he dissing your job? What is there to be embarrassed about, anyway? Collecting poo and then paddling it here and there makes a lot of sense.

The collection of human waste helps keep Tenochtitlan clean. Rich city dwellers may have their own privies. Others use public toilets, little huts set up along the streets. One scholar thinks that some of these toilets might have been built over flat-bottomed boats floating in the canal. When a boat is full, you paddle it through the canals to the *chinampas*. Farmers buy the manure to spread on their fields as fertilizer. Tanners are also interested in buying your smelly cargo. "Waste not, want not" could be an Aztec motto.

Aqueduct Builder

Every city needs clean water for its citizens. In the Maya city of Sayil, people collected rainwater and stored it in underground tanks because there were few springs or rivers in their region. As late as the 1800s, Londoners were still drinking the polluted water from the Thames River. But in the early 1400s, you and your engineering team are already hard at work on a way to bring fresh water from springs on the mainland to Tenochtitlan. Lake Texcoco's water is too full of minerals washed down from the mountains for drinking, bathing, or irrigating gardens. You have one big problem to solve, though. How do you transport water across water?

For many years in other areas of Mesoamerica, people have been building aqueducts to carry water from irrigation canals across streams. The aqueducts are hollowed-out logs supported by wooden trestles. Your solution takes this a giant step further. You put together a large work crew to build a series of small islands. The laborers anchor reed mats to the lake bottom about 3 to 4 m (10 to 13 feet) apart. Then they pile rocks, mud, and earth onto the rafts until they sink, forming a solid base for the 5-km (3-mile) aqueduct. Other workers make a trough lined with packed clay along the top of each island and connect the troughs with hollowed-out tree trunks. A path and plank bridges alongside the aqueduct allow people to cross the lake on the same structure used to carry the water. Water sellers in canoes collect the water in pottery containers at certain places along the aqueduct and sell it to city dwellers.

CHAPTER 2

Pyramid-Temple Building Jobs

The Mesoamericans built the largest pyramids outside Egypt. Why did they build them? Some scholars suggest that ancient people understood the scientific connection between mountains, the rising and setting sun, and seasonal rains. In an agricultural society, rain is crucial for survival. The mountain-like monuments, built facing west, could be used to track the sun's position and the coming of the rainy season. The flat-topped pyramids also served as platforms for temples and the performance of rituals. Everyone in the plaza below could watch what was happening on the stage far above them.

One of the most famous pyramid-temples in Mesoamerica is Tenochtitlan's Tempo Mayor. Since 1978, teams of archeologists have uncovered masks, jewelry, vases, and hundreds of other offerings to the gods in the area surrounding the buried remains of the temple in Mexico City. In another part of Mesoamerica, archeologists have discovered the Tarascan Empire's main temple complex. Its enormous platform supported five pyramid-temples, one honoring the sun god and four honoring his brothers, who held up the sky and the four ends of the world.

Restored pyramid-temples can be visited across Mesoamerica today, but pollution is erasing the carvings on some of them. Sadly, the stone monuments the temple builders thought would last forever are no match for acid rain.

Chief Architect

A new king has come to power, and now is your chance to shine. Your job is to take a smallish pyramid-temple and supersize it, using the old pyramid as a base for the new one. The great size of your pyramid—over 100 steps to the temple on top—will surely please the gods and strike awe in all who see it.

As an architect, you use mathematics and design skills in your work. First you prepare sketches of the pyramid, and probably a small clay model, to show the king and his advisors. Once your plan is approved, you must put together a team of workers, from the highest-ranking sculptor to the lowest-ranking laborer. Building materials are supplied by the rulers of outlying towns. Work gangs from the city's *calpulli*, or neighborhoods, deliver the rubble and dirt that will enlarge the old "sacred mountain," plus the blocks of *tezontle* (a light volcanic rock) that will cover them. Supervising the building and decoration of a pyramid-temple is an important job for a noble in Mesoamerica. You are honored to have been chosen as chief architect.

My design features a magnificent west-facing temple.

Mural Painter

You paint murals in the style that has swept Mesoamerica. Human figures are cartoon-like—outlined in black, filled in with bright colors, and drawn with heads that are bigger than their bodies. Although you also paint murals on the walls of palace rooms and courtyards, your most important murals appear on the walls of the temple on top of the pyramid. The only people who can enter the temple are the king and his priests. Your deeply religious murals show the gods creating life, making rain, bringing death, or traveling through the different regions of the cosmos. Your artwork will help the priests honor the gods and communicate with them.

Sculptor

CHIP, CHIP, CHIP. Transforming a large block of basalt into the terrifying head of a snake is slow work. Metals like iron are unknown. You use chisels made of a harder stone than basalt, as well as wooden mallets and wedges. You must be patient and not take any shortcuts. Aztecs call this approach "nibbling away in this world." It would be easier, for example, to leave the underside of your sculpture uncarved. After all, no one will see it. But remember what you learned in school: "What is carved should be like the original and have life." You must free a powerful snake from the stone so that it can guard the bottom of the pyramid stairway. When you are finished, another artist will paint the sculpture in bright colors. Until then, keep on nibbling.

HOW MUCH WILL YOU BE PAID?

The Aztec emperor Motecuhzoma II hired 14 sculptors to work on a large statue. Before they began, he gave each of them 10 loads of gourds, clothing, some cotton, and some maize. After they finished the statue, they were each given two servants, more clothing, and some cocoa, salt, and pottery.

Quarry Worker

The Maya built their pyramid-temples with the limestone rock that was common in their region. Limestone is fairly soft compared to other rocks. It begins to harden once it is exposed to air and the water it contains starts to evaporate. You cut blocks of limestone from layers close to the surface. You pry the blocks loose from the bedrock, in the same way we pry a brownie loose from the pan with a knife. The blocks are transported to construction sites on rollers made of logs or by water on rafts.

Stonecutter

Even if ancient Mesoamericans had gyms, you wouldn't need to take out a membership. Working with stone all day makes you one fit fellow. The *tezontle* blocks have been roughly "dressed," or shaped, at the quarry. Your job is to give them their final shape for the new pyramid-temple. Like the sculptor, yours is a chiseling, chipping job. Expect some smashed fingernails and a few scrapes and bruises.

A PYRAMID-TEMPLE'S MYSTERIOUS ECHO

The Maya built a 24-m-high (79-foot) pyramid-temple at Chichén Itzá on the Yucatán Peninsula in the Early Postclassic period. They named it after their quetzal-feathered serpent god, Kukulkan-Quetzalcoatl. (In several Meso-american cultures, the high-soaring red-breasted quetzal bird with its long green tail feathers was connected with the sky-god Quetzalcoatl.) At the spring equinox, a snakelike shadow zigzags down the pyramid as the rising sun's rays hit the edges of the monument. Today, if you clap your hands in front of the pyramid's stairs, you will hear a remarkable chirplike echo. Did the architects build the steps in such a way that the echo sounds like the sacred quetzal? Or is it, as some historians believe, just a coincidence?

You can hear the quetzal's call at this National Geographic website: http://animals.national geographic.com/animals/birds/quetzal.html.

Plasterer

Like the ancient Greeks and Romans, Meso-americans discovered that burning pieces of limestone produced a substance called quick-lime, or calcium oxide. When mixed with sand and water, it produces plaster. You are skilled at smoothing plaster quickly onto a wall with a trowel before the water in it evaporates, return-ing the material to its original form—calcium carbonate, or limestone. (You're a chemist and didn't even know it.)

Stonemasons use a similar mixture as mortar to glue the pyramid-temple's blocks together. Some scholars think that, in addition to providing a smooth surface for painting, the ancient Mesoamericans may have covered their stone monuments with plaster to protect them from torrential rains and hot, humid weather.

Laborer

If you're afraid of heights, you might want to look elsewhere for work. As the pyramid stair-ways are built, you and your fellow laborers haul the finished blocks up the stairs to their places in the platform walls. The ancient Mesoamericans didn't have horses or oxen, so you do all the heavy lifting and hauling of construction materials. Teamwork is very important. Making a human chain, for example, where materials or water containers are passed from one worker to another until they reach their destination, saves time and energy on the busy site.

CHAPTER 3

Palace Jobs

Just as the pyramid-temple was the center of religious life in an ancient Mesoamerican city-state, the roomy stone palace was the center of government. The ruler, his family, and high-ranking nobles lived in second-floor apartments. Scribes and government officials worked in offices on the first floor. High priests visited to consult the king on upcoming ceremonies. Expert craftspeople made luxury goods in the king's workshops. Merchants presented their finest wares, which were placed in the tribute storage rooms. And servants and slaves worked to keep everyone fed and happy. In short, the palace showed the social pyramid in action.

Great King

LISTEN!

You are one of three Aztec *huey tlatoani*, or great kings, one for each city of the Triple Alliance—Texcoco, Tlacopan, and Tenochtitlan. On your coronation day, you were told, "You are no longer a human being like us." Mesoamericans believe that the sacred forces in the world are present in people of high rank, as well as in animals, mountains, trees, and storms. As a great king, you are so godlike that commoners are not even allowed to look at you. In public, you wear an elaborate headdress, gold and greenstone ear-spools (large pierced earrings), jeweled lip rings, gold bands on your arms and legs, and a shimmering costume. Everything you wear radiates light, underlining your connection to the gods. Don't even think of letting anyone see you in your favorite old loincloth and cape.

In the *Florentine Codex*, Spanish friar Bernardino de Sahagún listed your duties. They include "war," "singing and dancing," "the ball court," "the installing of lords," "[ensuring] that payment to the gods be made," "the guarding of the city," "removing filth from the roads," and "the assembling of the seasoned warriors." Do you think you'll have enough time to enjoy your garden and zoo?

Juggler

You perform for the royal family and their guests. Your best trick is juggling a log with your feet while lying on your back. Other performers in your troupe dance on stilts or with a second person balanced on their shoulders. An Aztec juggler was among several acrobats taken in 1529 to perform in Madrid at the court of King Charles I of Spain. Royal courts throughout Mesoamerica and around the world enjoyed these types of performances.

"What is a blue-green jar filled with popcorn? The sky."
— Aztec riddle

Poet

Cuicani is the Nahuatl word for "poet" and "singer." Aztec poetry, known as "flowers and song," is usually sung or accompanied by music. You have been hired by the king to perform for the court and during festivals. You write and sing songs about the gods, heroic warriors, battles, and victories.

Tlatoani means "speaker," and, like all nobles, kings were expected to speak well and wisely. King Nezahualcoyotl of Texcoco was one of the most famous Aztec poets. He wrote beautiful, often sad poems about how precious and fleeting life is. Several women poets are also known, including Macuilxochitzin, the daughter of a Tenochtitlan royal advisor, whose song celebrates the life of a ruler.

"My flowers will not come to an end, my songs will not come to an end, I, the singer, raise them up: they are scattered, they are bestowed."
— King Nezahualcoyotl

Queen

Princess

You have been trained by your mother to be a household manager. Like the other royal wives, you don't get your hands dirty gathering herbs from the garden, cleaning the many rooms of the royal apartment, chucking wood on the fire, filling the baths with fresh water, or grinding maize for tortillas. You have dozens of servants for those chores. An important part of your job is passing on your skills to your daughters. You show them how to spin and weave cloth well and how to prepare food properly—lessons taught by both high-born and low-born mothers across Mesoamerica.

Would you like to sleep in or talk to your pet parrot rather than learn how to weave? If the answer is yes, you are on your way to becoming a bad noblewoman, someone who is described as "useless" and "a sleepy-head." Probably, though, you are looking forward to learning how to weave on the backstrap loom, a Meso-american invention that is still used today. Little girls can spin fiber into thread, but only teenage girls can be weavers.

Outside, in one of the many enclosed court-yards of the palace, your mother attaches one end of the loom to a post. She shows you how to wrap the strap on the other end around your

Grind the maize. Sweep the floors. Clean the house. Cook the dinner. GO!

hips. You must be strong enough to lean back and keep the lengthwise warp threads straight while you weave the weft threads under and over them. It's an important skill to learn. When you marry and have your own family, they will depend on you to make fine cotton cloth for clothing, ritual costumes, blankets, gifts, and temple hangings.

Speaking of future husbands: If you're superstitious, don't eat standing up. Otherwise, it is said that you will marry someone who lives far away. Oh, sorry, we forgot you are a king's daughter. Munch away standing on one leg. It won't really matter. Your father probably *will* marry you off to a young nobleman in a distant town, to cement the relationship between your city-state and your new husband's.

"Open your eyes to the way to be an artisan, to be a feather worker; to make designs by embroidering, to judge colors, to apply colors to please your sisters, your ladies, the noblewomen."
— Aztec noble to daughter, *Florentine Codex*

Embroiderer

Your skill as a textile artist has brought you great respect in the royal household. Although patterns can be woven into cloth, you stitch colorful butterflies, flowers, and eagles onto the king's special clothing with a bone or cactus-thorn needle. The shiny threads you use are made from the finest rabbit fur. Capes covered with your exquisite teeny-tiny-stitched designs are as highly prized as fine jewelry. Only kings are allowed to wear them in Aztec society. It's too bad that your king never wears the same cape twice (at least in public), but it means you're never out of work.

I think I've finally got the hang of this, Mom!

Prince

As the son of an Aztec king, you may think you will be able to do anything you please. Think again. The Aztecs had strict rules of etiquette for their children to follow. One nobleman gave his son these do's and don'ts: Don't spend too much time sleeping or daydreaming; don't stare at people; and don't gossip. Do come when you're called; do walk quietly; do tie your cape properly; and do eat slowly (no gulping your food like a dog). Just in case you forget to be polite when you're out in public, a servant will go along with you to remind you to bow and show respect to your elders.

Prime Minister

Along with hundreds of other nobles, you help run the Aztec Empire in the palace's special government rooms. As the *cihuacoatl*, you are the great king's second-in-command. This makes you very powerful. You organize military campaigns and serve as the chief justice of the supreme court.

Commoners may have difficulty understanding you sometimes. In the special way nobles talk to one another, you sometimes lie to be polite. For instance, you might thank another lord for his gift by saying, "You are a great lord. It really wasn't necessary for you to give me this wonderful cape." Every noble in the room, however, knows that you are much more important than the gift-giver and would be insulted if he had not presented you with a magnificent cape.

Do bow lower!

Ambassador

Just as today's British ambassadors represent their queen in countries around the world, you represent your king. To do this properly, you must be a high-ranking noble, one of the king's most trusted advisors. When you travel, you feel right at home in most of the city-states of the Triple Alliance empire. Their nobles have copied some Aztec clothing styles, manners, and customs and may even speak the Nahuatl language. When you visit independent city-states, though, your job is more difficult. You must convince the rulers and nobles of these states to become tributaries to the empire.

How do you go about this? First, you present a splendid gift to the foreign ruler. As a sign of respect, you take off your sandals and cover your richly decorated clothes with a plain cape. However, as a powerful Aztec ambassador, you usually get your way (most kings don't want to see their towns destroyed). If the king doesn't want to pay tribute to your ruler, he will send you home with an angry message and war will be declared. Then it is your job to take gifts to allied rulers to gain their support in the war effort.

Astronomer

Like most early peoples, Mesoamericans believed that the journeys of the stars and planets across the sky represented supernatural forces, or gods. As an astronomer, or starwatcher, you mark down the positions of the sun, moon, stars, and planets each day in relation to a building, a mountain, or a marker set in the ground. You use these records to compile calendars.

Ancient Mesoamericans had two main cycles of time—a 260-day sacred calendar for planning religious rituals and a 365-day solar calendar. The two fit together like the gears on a bicycle chain to give a combined date. Once every 18,980 days (365 days x 52 years), the first day of each calendar reappeared and the cycle began again.

Your skill as a timekeeper makes you a high-ranking person in the kingdom. Calendars help people plan farming, hunting, fishing, and other activities related to the seasons.

WRITING WITHOUT WORDS

Mesoamericans invented one of the first forms of writing in the world. Rather than an alphabet, they used pictures for objects or ideas. Today, we still use pictograms to make it easy for people who don't speak the same language to find the washroom, a hotel, or a restaurant.

It's easy to draw a temple to mean "temple," but how did Mesoamericans get across an idea? Sometimes they used an object that was connected to an idea; for example, a burning temple stood for "victory" and a trail of footprints meant "travel." The Mixtec language includes many words that have the same sound but are pronounced using different tones. Their scribes could simply draw the picture of an object whose name sounded the same as the idea.

In addition to pictograms, the Maya used pictures that stood for language sounds, usually syllables. For example, the Maya Yucatec word for "jaguar" is *balam*. The scribes combined the syllable signs for "ba," "la," and "ma" to make a hieroglyph.

Just as English is the language of business around the world today, in Postclassic times the Mixtec and Aztec writing systems could be read by speakers of different languages, since they used fewer phonetic glyphs and more pictures than other forms of writing. Their style of picture writing appeared in books, ceramics, and mural paintings across Mesoamerica.

Painter-Scribe

Do you like the colors black and red? We hope so, because they are the main colors artist-writers like you use to record your people's history, religion, and finances. In Mesoamerican culture, these colors symbolize knowledge or wisdom. Even the Aztec words for "writing," *in tlilli in tlapalli*, mean "the black, the red." Although both noble boys and noble girls learn to read and write, most scribes are men.

You write with a fine dog's-hair paintbrush on single sheets of paper, on large cotton sheets, on animal hides, and in books folded like

Royal Historian

accordions. Today writers capture the spoken word on the page in sentences, but you get your ideas across with pictures, symbols, and hieroglyphs. This system has worked well since the time of the Olmec, as early as 900 BCE. In fact, the Aztecs believe that the world itself was created by a divine artist who painted it into existence in a book. This makes the painter-scribe, or *tlacuilo*, the artist closest to the gods. You copy the "artwork" of the gods and create books of great spiritual beauty.

The king and his advisors depend on you for advice. You are a *tlamatini*, which means "knower of things." Now a wise old priest, you have learned the history of your people and all their sacred myths and stories by heart. Sometimes you jog your memory by looking at the painted history books written by earlier generations of painter-scribes. They are kept in the "book house" attached to the palace.

Old men and women have an important part to play in your culture. They are admired for what they have experienced in their long lives. No one would ever make fun of you for being old.

NOBLE AZTEC PERKS
- Only nobles can build a two-story house.
- Only nobles can pass their land on to their children.
- Only nobles can show off the most valuable luxury goods.
- Only nobles can wear decorated cotton capes.
- Only nobles can wear their capes below their knees.
- Only nobles can have more than one wife.

Servant

Like all Mesoamerican girls, you were taught how to grind maize for tortillas, a thin, pancake-like bread. You use the oldest kitchen tools in the Americas—a stone metate and a mano, which is like a rolling pin without handles. After you strip the kernels from the cobs, you soak them overnight in water mixed with powdered limestone. You are now ready to grind the wet kernels into dough.

Because you work in the palace, you use one of the new three-legged metates. You kneel with the higher single leg closest to you and use the mano to grind the corn with a downward back-and-forth motion. You can push harder against the kernels on its sloping stone surface than on the flat surface of your grandmother's metate. Next, you pat the dough from hand to hand to shape it into a circle. You cook it on a round clay griddle over the fire.

Everyone, from kings to slaves, eats tortillas. A king's may be wrapped around spicy cooked turkey or exotic seafood; commoners like you dip theirs in a simple chili sauce.

Cook

A good cook is described as "energetic," "one who likes good food," and "[one] who washes her hands." A bad cook is "sweaty," "stuffed," and "very much a commoner." Since you work in the palace, you must be very, very good.

Mesoamericans probably ate twice a day, once in the morning and once in the afternoon. On special days when no one is allowed to eat for religious reasons, you get a day off. But on all the other days, the royal cooks must prepare meals for the hundreds of people who live and work in the palace. When banquets are held during religious holidays, even more people must be fed. Sometimes freelance cooks are hired for these events; for example, male cooks might have dug pits and barbecued meat on criss-crossed sticks placed over a fire.

The day of a feast, which begins at midnight, you work from early morning on through the night. It is hard *not* to become sweaty as you roast chilis, cook stews, stir sauces, and boil beans, not to mention plucking feathers from birds and steaming maize dough in corn husks to make tamales. Your specialty, though, is a frog casserole with green chili.

CHAPTER 4

Food and Drink Jobs

Agricultural jobs made many other jobs possible in Mesoamerica. Growing maize, vegetables, and fruit, and raising turkeys, allowed people to settle down in one area. Farming not only gave people a more reliable food supply than hunting and gathering alone provided, but also gave them the time to plan cities, build pyramids, write poetry, and make pottery, jewelry, cloth, and other objects. However, that doesn't mean farmers could supply enough food for everyone. Mesoamericans still hunted, fished, and gathered foods that some of us would find disgusting today, from crunchy grasshoppers to juicy worms.

Hill Farmer

Since you don't have oxen or horses to help you plow your fields, you do all the work yourself, using simple hand tools. You turn over the soil with a shovel-like wooden tool, dig planting holes with a pointed wooden stick, and prune and harvest with a simple knife.

In hilly areas, you build stone walls across the hills, then dig into the hillside behind the new wall to make a flat area, or terrace, for growing maize and beans. These steplike fields capture rainwater in the soil, so that it doesn't just flow down the hill. On more gentle slopes, farmers use long rows of maguey (agave) plants grown close together as a low terrace wall.

Slave

During the four-year drought and famine of the 1450s, some Aztecs sold themselves to the Totonac people for 400 to 500 cobs of maize to feed their families. Others sold their children into slavery. You became "someone's digging stick," as the Aztecs would say, because a farmer caught you stealing some maize from his field. Under both Maya and Aztec law, he had the right to enslave you. You now have to work off your debt to him.

Landless Farm Laborer

You work on land belonging to a nobleman. Similar to the serfs in medieval Europe, you are tied to his land and can't work anywhere else. One of your duties is to provide your lord with wood and water. If you are an expert with a sling, expect to be assigned to a lookout post in a maize field. It's your job to scare away the birds and raccoons. (The raccoon's name, *mapachtli*, is also the word for "thief.") And you thought only stuffed shirts could be scarecrows!

THE DAILY GRIND

"Maize" is a New World name for the plant *Zea mays*, or "Indian corn," as it is sometimes called. The Nahuatl word for it, *teocintli*, means "food of the gods." Europeans of this era ate wheat, the Chinese ate rice, and the Mesoamericans ate maize every day. You could eat any of these grains and feel full; without them, you could easily starve.

To hear the sound that most children woke up to in the morning, take two rocks, one roundish and one flat, and rub one against the other. That raspy noise is the sound the mano made grinding the maize kernels on the metate.

Chinampa Farmer

You work in the *chinampas*, or "floating gardens," of Tenochtitlan. These narrow, rectangular agricultural fields, made from reclaimed swampland along Lake Texcoco's shores, rise about 1 m (3 feet) above water level. You and your family, who live in a tiny house on your plot, grow a wide variety of edible and medicinal plants, including maize, squash, tomatoes, beans, and some flowers. Growing seedlings in special beds and using fertilizer and mulch—all techniques that will be used by modern gardeners—make you highly successful. You and your fellow farmers are so successful, in fact, that parts of the lake disappear under a network of fields and canals.

Farmer's Wife

Like all commoner women, you begin your day before sunrise, spending four to five hours grinding maize on your metate. (Any longer and the palms of your hands would be ground up too.) The rest of your day is spent spinning and weaving, cleaning, cooking over the smoky fire, and caring for your children—and for your turkeys, if you have any. On market days, you visit the local market to sell your produce or the goods you have made.

Who takes out the garbage? You do, but there's very little to remove from your one-room house. Leftover vegetable and fruit skins are used to fertilize your garden. You toss broken pottery into the backyard, where your children have fun playing with it.

Woodcutter

People need fuel to cook their meals and to heat their homes. Potters, goldsmiths, and other craftspeople also need firewood, as do priests for their ritual fires. As populations in Meso-america grow, fuel becomes scarce and has to be brought from farther away. You sell four types. Wood and charcoal are your first-grade fuels. Your second-grade fuel includes sunflower stalks, dried maize stalks, and large dried maguey leaves. These stalks and leaves are used mainly for reheating food, because they don't provide the consistent, long-burning heat needed for cooking. They also produce more smoke than wood does. Kindling—small branches used to light a fire—is your third category. Noble families buy your fourth, premium-quality product—pine bark, the firewood of the gods. They like its scent and the beautiful flames it makes.

While you're in the forest, you might as well collect some resin, or sticky sap, from the copal tree for incense. No ritual is complete without it, so you can expect a steady stream of customers. Stone-mosaic makers will also buy your resin to use as a glue.

Pulque Maker

Mesoamericans made several drinks from juicy plants, including palm wine and a pineapple drink. Your alcoholic drink is made from maguey sap. Like maple trees, maguey plants don't pro-duce sap year-round. You have to wait until the maguey is about to sprout a flower shoot. Then you cut out the bud and the middle of the plant. This leaves a large hole that fills up with sweet, milky-looking juice, which you suck out into a hollow gourd and empty into a jar twice daily over a period of several months.

To make pulque, you add some microorganisms to ferment the juice, in the same way yeast is used to make beer. Although it smells a bit like bananas when it is first made, pulque can become stinky if it isn't drunk within a few days. In fact, its Spanish name may come from the Nahuatl word *poliuhqui*, which means "decom-posed." (In Nahuatl, the drink is called *octli*.) Once you have removed the last drop of sap, the plant is all pulqued out—forever. Be sure to replace the dead magueys with new shoots. They will root in the soil, producing a fresh crop of magueys to tap when the time is right.

Salt Maker

For many centuries, your ancestors have traded salt. Salt is used to preserve seafood and animal flesh, to make food taste better, to make dyes for cloth, and to clean teeth. In pre-Hispanic times, salt was scarce and difficult to produce, which made it very valuable.

You work as a salt maker in the driest months on the southwest Pacific coast, from April to June. In the rainy season, you fish or work in the fields. You need lots of sunlight for your work. Sunny weather shrinks the nearby estuary, leaving a salty crust on the beach. You dig up the soil, run ocean water through it, and pour this salty mixture, called brine, into shallow, lime-coated pools. The sun evaporates the brine, leaving behind salt crystals. Centuries later, archeologists will be able to see where you did your work by the large mounds of leached soil you leave behind.

If you work in the Valley of Mexico, you find your salt in the soil around saline lakes. Some historians believe that in the twelfth century, makers in the region developed a new way to produce salt crystals. Instead of the sun-evaporation method, you boil the brine over a fire in a roofed shelter to extract the salt. This makes it possible to produce salt in the rainy season and yields a better-quality, fine-grained salt. You use so many clay pots to transport your salt that the region's potters begin making a special type just for your industry. However, you must compete with the makers of the finest salt of all, brought from the Yucatán Peninsula and said to look like diamonds.

CHAPTER 5

Everyday Crafts Jobs

The raw materials Mesoamericans used to make everyday objects remained the same over many generations—maguey plant fibers, clay, stone, rubber, reeds, and wood. In the Postclassic period, though, new ways to use some of those materials were developed. The three-legged metate was designed, as well as new basins and strainers for preparing dried corn. A clay griddle allowed cooks to prepare tortillas in much the same way they are prepared today. Many everyday crafts jobs were part-time, carried out by farmers and their wives and children on patios or in the yard under a shady tree.

Blade Maker

You will definitely be caught "knapping" on this job. That's not to suggest it's a lazy man's job, though. Far from it. "Knapping" means flaking and shaping rock. It is a highly skilled craft, which you might have learned in a knapping school at the nearby quarry.

You craft blades for knives and razors from a jet-black volcanic glass called obsidian, which is also used to make mirrors. Most of your blades, which range in length from 10 to 15 cm (4 to 6 inches), have even sharper edges than modern blades. Here's one way scholars think you might have made the larger ones. First, use a small hammer-stone to shape a chunk of obsidian into a cone; that will make it easier to fracture. Sit on the ground and place the prepared "core" between

your heels in a shallow pit with the flat end facing you. Then, put one end of the blade making tool's pole under your bellybutton against the wide cloth belt worn around your hips. Bending forward, place the notch of the tool's blade remover between two ridges on the edge of the core. Holding the long pole with both hands, push forward with your abdominal muscles and pull up on the handle in one smooth motion, lifting a sharp sliver in the form of a blade from the core.

Blade making is a bit like splitting a log into firewood with an ax. If you don't hit the log at the right angle to the wood's grain with just the right amount of force, the wood won't split. As in all crafts, practice is the only way to improve your skill, so get knapping!

Maguey Worker

You and the other women and girls in your community are maguey spinners and weavers. But before you can do either of these jobs, you work together to remove the fibers from the cactus-like leaves of the maguey plant. (Maguey sure comes in handy—it's a fiber, it's a fuel, it's a drink, it's a wonder plant!)

First, you soften the thick leaf by pounding it on a flat stone. Then, you use a scraper to remove the pulp from the fiber (think of the threads in a piece of celery). Only a tiny part of the leaf is fiber, so this is a big, wet, messy job with a lot of cleanup afterward. The fiber is dried for several hours in the sun, then straightened and cleaned with one of the plant's large spines. Or, if you have a barrel cactus handy, you can pull the mass of fibers over its spiny top to get rid of tangles. Another way you can process the maguey is to cook the leaves in a fire, using dead maguey roots as fuel, and then bury the leaves in a pit for several days to rot the fleshy part. This makes it easier to scrape the leaves, but the fiber is darker in color.

Spinner

What job can you do while walking to a friend's house? What job uses one of the first machines ever made by humans? And what job lets you drop something over and over again without getting fired? Spinning.

When you were only four, your mother or grandmother taught you how to spin the maguey plant's fibers into thread using a drop spindle. The spindle has two main parts: a wooden stick and a whorl, which is a baked-clay circular weight. To spin, you first use your fingers to twist together a beginning length of yarn from the fibers. You attach this "leader" to the stick above the whorl. Holding on to the leader and fiber with one hand, you drop the spindle and give it a spin. You then feed the fibers through your fingers as the weight of the whorl pulls the fibers down and the spinning motion twists them into thread. When the spindle hits the ground, you pick it up and wind the newly spun thread around it. Then you drop it again and again and again, all the way to Citlalmina's house.

The thick maguey-fiber thread you create is used to make fishing nets and to weave clothing for commoners and sturdy cloths for carrying goods and produce. Finer threads, made from the innermost leaves of the maguey, are used to make baby-carrying cloths.

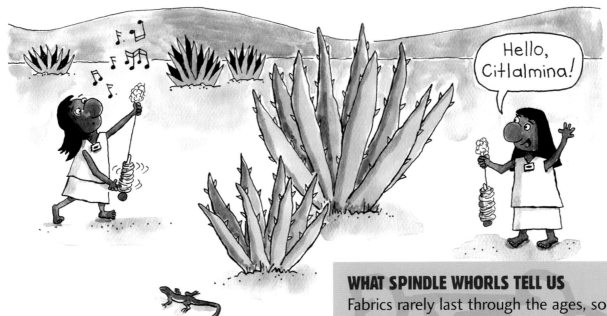

Hello, Citlalmina!

"The poor people dressed in henequen, which is a thick thread made of maguey, and the rich people dressed in cotton, with an embroidered border of feathers and rabbit fur."
— Juan de Torquemada, *Monarchia Indiana*, 1615

WHAT SPINDLE WHORLS TELL US

Fabrics rarely last through the ages, so how can archeologists tell what ancient people in a certain area wore or spun for trade? One way is to weigh spindle whorls. In Mesoamerica, whorls weighing under 11 g (0.4 ounces) were used to spin cotton, those between 11 and 30 g (0.4 and 1 ounce) were used for spinning fine maguey fiber, and those over 30 g (1 ounce) were used for spinning coarse maguey fibers.

Potter

If you were a workshop potter, you would make pottery for noble families—bowls, cocoa cups, serving dishes, and plates. You would decorate your work with the latest designs—spots with dots, circles with dots, wavy lines, and shapes that look like maguey thorns.

Well, forget that. You don't have time for the fancy stuff. You're a part-time potter who makes plain, everyday kitchen vessels—pots for cooking beans and soaking maize, big jars for storing water, and round griddles for cooking tortillas. You use strips of clay to build your pots by hand, because no one in the Americas owns a potter's wheel yet. When it's time to "fire" your soft clay pots, you and the other potters in your village save on fuel by firing your pots together in one big outdoor fire. You trade any extra pots you make for other goods at the local market.

Adobe Brick Maker

Like the village women who create everyday pottery, you and some of the other farmers of your village work part-time making clay-and-straw, or adobe, bricks for sale in the regional market. The bricks are formed in wooden frames, turned out to dry in the sun, and then fired. Adobe is such a useful, easy-to-make construction material that even pyramids have been built of it.

Clay Figurine Maker

For many centuries, Mesoamericans have made small clay sculptures. You use clay molds to make figurines of gods, people, animals, and birds. Your workshop may also make blowgun pellets, rattles, and spindle whorls. The trick is knowing when to remove the objects from their molds for firing. Not enough drying in the sun and they will collapse; too much and they will crack.

Some of your unpainted figurines may be placed in a special spot in private homes to honor the gods, just as some Christians today display a small statue of Jesus or Buddhists an image of Buddha. Other figures may be used in healing rituals by midwives or healers. By the time your figurines are found by archeologists around an ancient house, they have often been beheaded. This might mean they were broken on purpose in a sacred ritual.

WHO NEEDS TATTOOS?

Ceramic stamps with geometric or animal designs are sometimes found at archeological sites in the Valley of Mexico. Researchers believe people may have used them with paint to decorate their bodies or possibly their clothing. Would you like one of a Fire Serpent? A snake with fiery arrows shooting from its mouth was found on five stamps at an archeological site at Chiconautla, a Postclassic town that paid tribute to Texcoco, the Triple Alliance city ruled by the famous Nezahualcoyotl in the 15th century.

Rope Maker

Doing this job would make anyone a little twisted: you twist maguey fibers into rope. You make thin cords by rolling the fibers against your thigh by hand. For thick ropes, you and a partner use a "rope walk." At one end of this path, you set up a large wooden disk. Strands from a bundle of fiber are attached to it. As one of you turns the disk, the other walks with the fiber, twisting the strands into rope.

Your craft is an ancient one in Mesoamerica. In the seventh century, the Maya built what may have been the longest rope suspension bridge in the world at that time. The rope has long since disappeared, but the remains of stone piers indicate that the bridge stretched 100 m (600 feet) across the Usumacinta River at the city of Yaxchilán.

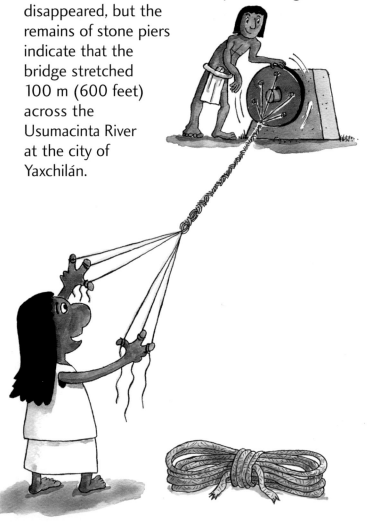

Paper Maker

You are a farmer who works part-time making paper from maguey fibers. You would be very surprised to see people today wiping their noses with paper. What a snotty thing to do! To you, paper is a substance of great worth. It is used not only to make books but also for burning in ritual offerings.

If you lived in another region in Mesoamerica, you would make paper from the inner bark of a wild fig tree. After soaking the bark strips in water, you lay them out in a grid pattern and beat the fibers with a mashing stone attached to a wooden handle. You add a gummy material and use the bark beater again. Your pounding spreads the fibers into a thin sheet of paper. To make folded accordion-style books, you glue the dried sheets together into strips. *Amoxtli*, the Nahuatl word for "book," comes from *amatl* ("paper") and *oxitl* ("pine gum").

Metate and Mano Maker

Every household in Mesoamerica has used your product since about 2000 BCE. In fact, grinding stones are so common that there are sayings about them. If small children lick any leftover maize dough off the metate, their mothers warn them that their teeth will break and fall out. (Actually, grit from the stone could wear down and chip teeth, so, as usual, mothers did know best!) If the metate itself breaks, it is a warning that someone in the family will die soon.

In hilly or mountainous areas, you look for a particular type of granite for your metates—one that is coarse but will not crumble or become too smooth with constant use. You can tell by the color of the rock whether it is top quality. Brownish, greenish, or purplish granites make the best metates. Basalt is also used.

The first step is to remove a slab of stone from the bedrock. Since you only have hand tools, it can take all day to make just one cut. Once the slab is removed, you split it into smaller pieces. You trace the shape of the metate onto one of the pieces to guide your blows. Making the three legs is the tricky part. One misplaced blow can ruin your metate— a two-legged metate is useless.

The mano is cut from the same stone and is a little shorter than the finished metate is wide.

THE LATEST KITCHEN TOOL
In the 17th century, Mesoamerican stone metates were exported across the ocean so that chocolate-crazy Europeans could grind their cacao beans the proper way.

Rubber Ball Maker

One Aztec tribute record shows that up to 16,000 rubber balls were sent each year to Tenochtitlan from the hot, humid lowlands where you live. You make some of those popular balls. (You would have laughed at the leather, wood, or cloth balls of the Europeans of that time. What good is a ball if it doesn't bounce?) Not all of your balls are used in the popular ballgame that is played throughout Mesoamerica. Some are burned or buried as offerings to the gods.

To make rubber, you first need to remove the thick white stuff called latex from rubber trees. Historians don't know how you did this, but they think it was similar to the way your great-grandchildren would collect it in colonial times. You cut the bark of the tree so that the latex underneath flows down a channel to the ground, where you collect it. Out in the air the latex thickens and turns gray. When you boil it with certain plant juices or roots, it thickens even more, and long elastic threads separate from the rest of the mixture. You roll these soft strips of rubber into balls—or shape them into tips for drumsticks, sandal bottoms, and small figurines used in festivals.

Another tree that ancient Mesoamericans tapped was the sapodilla tree. Its white resin was cooked and used to make chewing gum.

Mat Maker

Like many people living in semitropical or tropical climates around the world, you and your family sit and sleep on woven mats. Your father cuts reeds growing in the shallow water along the lakeshore. You help your mother dry the reeds in the sun for about a week, then tie them up in bundles ready for weaving into mats and baskets. To make a mat, you weave the reeds together and pound each row with a stone to keep it flat.

Unlike cloth mattresses and chairs, reed mats stay cool when it is hot. You feel sorry for poorer families who only have a platform of dirt to sleep on in their huts. You don't feel sorry for the preteen Aztec boys whose parents make them lie on wet mats as punishment for their bad behavior. Instead, you feel sorry for their parents for having such "thick-heads" as sons.

Broom Maker

Cooking over a wood fire makes a mess. Ashes, slivers of wood, droppings from the house mouse—all have to be cleaned up. That is why one of the most common sounds in your community is the swish, swish, swish of brooms. When a young Aztec woman marries, one piece of advice the elders give her is to "take care of the sweeping." Sweeping is not simply a household chore. It is also a religious ritual performed by women and priests alike to bring order to the world. During the harvest festival of Ochpaniztli (Road Sweeping) in September, people sweep the temples, public buildings, and roads—a sort of spring cleaning in the fall.

Some ancient brooms were simply branches tied together. Your straw broom is much better than a bunch of twigs at sweeping and is not much different from the ones that would be sold hundreds of years later. You gather the straw, choose the straightest pieces, trim them, and then attach them to a broomstick. You won't have any trouble selling your brooms in the market if they're well made.

Canoe Builder

You build the dugout canoes that are the most popular boats in Mesoamerica. In addition to carrying goods, food, and people from place to place, they are used for fishing and even hunting. In the winter, when migrating ducks and geese arrive on the Valley of Mexico's lakes, hunters string nets on poles over the water. At dusk they go out in their canoes and scare the birds, forcing them to fly into the nets.

Archeologists believe the seagoing Maya of the Yucatán Peninsula made canoes that were 15 m (50 feet) long and 2 m (7 feet) wide. Without metal tools, it would take a chipping long time to hollow out a tree trunk for a canoe that size.

CHAPTER 6

Luxury Crafts Jobs

In our culture, your parents may take a gift of wine or flowers to give to their hosts at a dinner party. More wine is produced and more flowers are grown because people give these items as presents. In Mesoamerica, gift-giving among the nobles kept entire crafts communities in business. Births, marriages, funerals, and ceremonies of various kinds all required the presentation of gifts, and once a gift was given, it had to be repaid.

In the Mixtec and Zapotec societies of southern Mexico, commoners were not allowed to wear jewelry. Even the production of luxury goods was restricted to the noble class, with most of it done by royal women. Kings married many wives not only to make alliances but also as a way to enrich themselves by trading their wives' creations for other luxury goods.

CONGRATULATIONS!

Goldsmith

Where does your "excrement" come from? (Bet that got your attention.) The Nahuatl word for "gold" means "excrement of the sun." Gold is shiny like the sun's rays, is the color of diarrhea—you get the idea. Like the 19th-century gold rush miners, ancient Mesoamericans panned for gold in streams and rivers. They turned the nuggets they found into jewelry, cups, and bowls.

The Mixtec are famous for their gold work using the lost-wax process. As a master Mixtec goldsmith, you have been given the honor of making a butterfly nose ornament for a lord. First, you make a bottom mold of powdered charcoal and potter's clay in the shape of the wings. After that has dried, you press a thin layer of beeswax and copal resin over the mold. You put the final touches on your design before covering it with a layer of moist clay. Before the clay mold on top dries out, you push a tube through it down to the wax layer. When the mold is baked at high temperatures, the wax runs out the tube. You pour melted gold down the tube to replace the wax, allow it to harden, then break the mold to reveal a butterfly fit for a noble nose.

Actually, this isn't even one of your more complicated pieces. You've made a gold lip-plug in the shape of a snake's head with tiny teeth and a tongue that moves. That makes today's fashion of piercing lips with a plain silver ring look a little tame, don't you think?

Butterflies are the latest fashion in Tenochtitlan.

MORE PRECIOUS THAN GOLD

If someone offered you a green jade bead or one made of pure gold, which would you choose? A Mesoamerican would choose the green bead. In Postclassic times, greenstones were much more precious than gold, partly because they were rare and partly because the color green stood for fertility and water. In fact, an Aztec metaphor for anything precious was *in chalchituitl in quetzalli*, or "the jade bead, the quetzal feather." Wearing greenstone jewelry let everyone know that you were a nobleman or a noblewoman.

Bell Maker

Feather Artist's Apprentice

While other Tarascan metalworkers make needles, fishhooks, tweezers, and rings by hammering cold metal into shape, you use the goldsmith's lost-wax technique to make your bells. In fact, when west Mexican cultures first began making metal objects, bells were the most common item made. Some of your small copper bells end up underground, worn around dead lords' necks, ankles, or wrists. Those are, of course, silent as the grave. But above ground, on dancers' ankle and wrist bands or on rattlesticks, the bells tinkle, jingle, and ring.

When city dwellers spot a feather today, it's usually a grimy pigeon or gull feather lying in the street. The last thing they want to do is touch it. But you can't wait until your father lets you begin working with the feathers in his workshop.

Your father "paints" with colored feathers in the same way a mural artist paints with colored pigments. Your mother and sisters dye the turkey and duck feathers that form the first layer of the mosaic he is making. You and your brothers prepare the glue that fastens the feathers to the cloth backing. The glue is made from the roots or bulblike, thickened stems of orchids. In the country, farmers dry the stems or roots in the sun, grind them into a powder, and then sell it in the market. You mix the powder with water to make a paste. For the mosaic's final layer, your father glues on the brilliant feathers imported from faraway tropical forests. The result is a shimmering ceremonial shield for a king or nobleman to carry.

When a bell's pebble or clay clapper hits the inside wall of the bell, the metal vibrates and produces sound waves. The type of sound, or pitch, the bell makes depends on its size and shape. Small bells produce a high-pitched "bing," large ones a low-pitched "bong." Gas bubbles can form in liquid copper and get trapped when the metal hardens, making a dull-sounding bell. But like other bell makers, you know how to prevent this from happening.

Wood Carver

You work with other craftsmen in the palace workshops, making gifts for noblemen visiting from the provinces, as well as objects for the king and his family and friends. You carve handles for the ceremonial shields made by feather workers and the bases for masks decorated by mosaic workers. One day you might be carving the head of a jaguar or an eagle into a shield's handle; another day you're teaching an apprentice how to make a beautiful rattle. Drums, gongs, statues of gods for the temples—you can carve them all. Let's face it, though, your work is not as highly valued as the work done by sculptors. Wood disappears, but stone lasts forever.

Mosaic Mask Maker

If you sometimes feel you have toes for fingers, you might want to skip this job. As a mosaic craftsman, you glue tiny squares of turquoise onto a wooden frame in the shape of a skull, using pieces of shell for teeth. Masks have a long tradition in Mesoamerica, stretching back to the Olmecs. They are worn in religious rituals or placed over the faces of dead kings before they are buried or cremated. The splendid death mask you're making is the face of the god the king represented in life. The king will wear it as he passes from the world of nature to the world of the spirit.

Shell Worker

Sure, you can make shell bracelets, earspools, and beads, but isn't that a waste of your talent? Like other Huastec shell workers, you are famous for your skill in creating big chest ornaments for men, called pectorals. That even sounds manly, doesn't it? Pectorals are worn by nobles and priests. You make yours by sawing giant conch shells into spiral sections. You may file the section into the shape of a flower or engrave scenes from Huastec myths on it. Your apprentice polishes the ornaments and at the end of the day sweeps up the shell bits on the floor so that they can be ground into lime.

Like many Mesoamerican luxury crafts, your pectorals have special meaning. The conch shell is the symbol for the wind god Ehecatl, who is often shown wearing a pectoral in painted books. The conch's spirals may have reminded people of swirling dust whipped up by the wind or the sound of the wind when they held the shell up to their ear.

This is one of my finest creations.

Flower Worker

You look as sweet as you smell!

The Aztecs really did take the time to smell the flowers. Flowers—from the giant sunflower to the tiny marigold—played an important part in Mesoamerican life. They were admired for their beauty and their fragrance. After choosing your flowers from the flower sellers in the market, you string them together to make long necklaces, head wreaths, or bracelets. These are worn by dancers during religious festivals and given to noble guests at feasts so that they can enjoy the scent before the food is served.

Many flowers were grown south of Tenochtitlan in the gardens of Xochimilco, which means "place of flowers." Today flowers are still grown in this World Heritage Site and taken by boat to Mexico City markets. At Christmas, boats carrying hundreds of thousands of poinsettias cause traffic jams on the canals. Similar slowdowns must have taken place before important Aztec festivals centuries ago.

CHAPTER 7

Trade and Market Jobs

Traveling merchants provided the raw material used by luxury craftspeople to make gifts for successful warriors and visiting allied kings, as well as prestige items for nobles to use or exchange among themselves. Regional merchants supplied local markets with practical goods such as salt, cacao beans, and cotton. Local people sold small amounts of extra maize, chilis, clothing, or whatever they produced.

Market day was a social event throughout Mesoamerica. In Tenochtitlan, the largest market was divided into streets according to the item sold. It was open every day, while the large city-state markets were held every five days (an Aztec week) and village and town markets even less frequently. No one could open a store in their neighborhood. People were allowed to sell their goods only in the market, under the watchful eye of the state. In fact, selling goods outside the market was said to anger the market god.

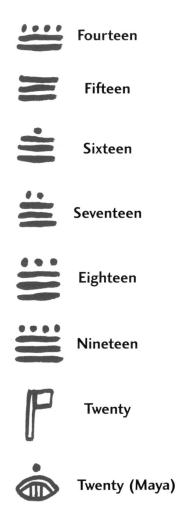

One
Two
Three
Four
Five
Six
Seven
Eight
Nine
Ten
Eleven
Twelve
Thirteen

Fourteen
Fifteen
Sixteen
Seventeen
Eighteen
Nineteen
Twenty
Twenty (Maya)

HOW TO COUNT, THE MESOAMERICAN WAY

To be a trader or seller, you had to know how to count. While we use multiples of 10 in our decimal system, the Mesoamericans added together their 10 fingers and 10 toes, resulting in 20. A dot • represented one and a bar — five. The Aztecs drew a flag for 20; the Maya drew a shell for zero and placed a dot above it to indicate 20. Either was far simpler than the arithmetic of the ancient Romans, who came up with seven symbols for numbers — I (1), V (5), X (10), L (50), C (100), D (500), M (1,000). Our own Arabic system uses nine symbols.

Long-Distance Merchant

"They traveled exhausted by the heat and the winds; they traveled exhausted; they went exhausted; they went sighing, walking wearily." Hmm, the Aztec elder who described the *pochteca*'s job to the friar Bernardino de Sahagún seems to think your work might be a little, shall we say, EXHAUSTING!

As a *pochteca* you do walk long distances, sometimes for several months, but it's not as though you have to carry your own goods. You have porters for that. On your travels, you sleep in shelters built along the trail. Maybe you are exhausted because you're afraid robbers or enemy warriors will swoop down on your caravan if you fall asleep. (Every evening you and your fellow traders make a temporary shrine to your patron god, Yacateuctli, and ask for his protection.) Or maybe you are exhausted because you're worried about getting lost. (You have a cloth map, though, showing roads, places you can cross rivers safely, and springs where you can get a drink.) Or maybe you are exhausted because you've been away from home for a long time and miss your family.

Porter

Does this describe you? You would rather take a piggyback ride than give one. You complain if your backpack has more than two books in it. You whine if you have to walk anywhere. If that sounds like you, you will not be a happy camper in this job.

As a *tlameme* you are the trucker and taxi driver of your day. But because you don't have wheels, you carry your cargo or fare on your back, supported by a strap around your forehead. You may be the slave of a long-distance trader. You and other porters carry his goods through shadowy pine forests, across fast-flowing rivers, and up mountain passes. Like today's hikers, you fall into a rhythm set by the first member of the group. As you walk, you watch out for thorny branches and smooth rocks slick with rain. Falling with about 11 kg (25 pounds) on your back is something you don't want to do.

Faster, men. FASTER!

River Boatman

INSTANT MEALS

Ancient Mesoamericans ate a type of food that has almost disappeared today. They added water and flavorings to ground maize kernels and made *atolli*, a thin porridgelike drink similar to European gruel of that time. Travelers carried ground toasted maize in a little sack; adding water made an instant meal.

You are a skilled Maya canoeist who is an expert at running the rapids through the canyons of the Usumacinta River. The river is one of several used as highways by traders to transport their goods. Unlike the northern birchbark canoe, which can be easily carried overhead along trails around rapids, your heavy dugout canoe must be dragged along a portage or pulled by ropes through rapids. This is why you would rather save the time and trouble and shoot the rapids. Let's face it, it's more fun, too.

Recently, traders have begun using large seagoing canoes to carry salt, cotton, honey, ceramics, jade objects, and other goods around the coast of the Yucatán Peninsula. This is cutting into your business. Their canoes can carry more goods than your river-going dugout.

Chocolate Seller

To make the expensive chocolate drink that you sell, you grind the cacao beans and mix them with warm water spiced up with chili peppers, spices, or even flowers. You are known for the tall "heads" of delicious foam on your slightly bitter drinks, which you produce by pouring the liquid back and forth from one container to another. Mesoamericans have been shaking it up for a thousand years, since the Maya first began making their version of this yummy drink, *kakaw*.

Sandal Seller

Looking at feet is another way to tell who's who in Mesoamerican society. The king wears fancy jewel-studded sandals made of jaguar skin with deerskin soles. Nobles, experienced warriors, and merchants wear much plainer sandals, and many commoners go barefoot. In fact, Motecuhzoma I would not allow anyone except his prime minister and himself to wear sandals in the palace. Like other Aztecs, you look down your nose at the yucca or palm sandals worn by nomads from the northern deserts who wander through the market.

   How are the maguey-fiber sandals you sell different from the ones worn elsewhere in the ancient world? Yours have a woven heel guard, which looks like the back of a shoe. Just the thing to protect your customers' heels from rocky trails, rattlesnakes, or nipping little dogs. How good is your design? Archeologists have found sandals dating from the Postclassic period in dry caves. They look very similar to the maguey-fiber sandals worn today by older women in Nahuatl communities. (Younger women find them too scratchy.)

Fruit and Vegetable Seller

Most Mesoamerican families living in villages, towns, or cities have a large garden beside their home. In yours you grow vegetables and herbs. You also have a few avocado trees. Avocados are one of your best sellers at the market. Mesoamericans eat a diet low in fat—no butter, no cheese, no milk, no bacon. The creamy green flesh of the avocado, though, contains large amounts of fatty oil. You and your customers mash it up with chopped tomatoes and onions to make *ahuaca-mulli*, what we call guacamole.

Dye Maker and Seller

You sell pigments in your market stall. These are colored substances that are mixed with a liquid to make cloth dyes, ink, and body paint. You buy *purpura pansa* from Pacific traders for your light purple dye. (The yellow body fluid of this shellfish turns to reddish purple when exposed to sunlight.) Mashed Spanish moss makes brown, pine tree soot makes black, and ground, heated limestone makes white. (Wow, that limestone is one all-purpose rock!)

Some of your dyes are absorbed by cloth without any help. Others are mixed with another substance called a mordant to fix the color and prevent it from running out of the fabric when it is washed. You make mordants from mineral salts and sell them alongside your dyes. Since pee mixed with lime is also used as a mordant, you could try selling your own as a jarful of super-duper dye fixer—but only if you're a very persuasive salesperson.

Counterfeiter

The beans of cacao trees, which grow in the tropical forests of southern Mesoamerica, are traded throughout the region. The farther they must be transported, the more people in distant markets have to pay for them. Only nobles drink the spicy chocolate drink made from them. Everyone, however, uses the almond-sized beans as money. (Other objects used as money include cotton capes, small T-shaped metal "axes," and feather quills filled with gold dust.) Around the time of the Spanish Conquest, a turkey egg cost three cacao beans; the entire bird cost 100 beans.

You make fake beans by removing the cacao beans from their coverings and replacing the beans with avocado pits or wax balls. You mix the counterfeit beans with real ones and hope no one will notice. Shame on you for breaking the law.

Market Officer

People who sell goods in the market at Tlatelolco, Tenochtitlan's sister city, have to pay a fee to your boss, the market superintendent. Your job is to make sure they don't try to cheat their customers by using measures that are smaller than they should be. You also watch out for thieves, sellers of stolen goods, and counterfeiters. Those who are arrested are tried in a special courthouse set up at the market. If they are found guilty of a minor crime, you place them in small wooden cages. In Tenochtitlan, those who sell stolen property are executed.

Slave Dealer

When they return home after a profitable trip, traveling merchants must pay their debt to the gods who made their success possible. They do this by buying slaves from you at a large market. The men and women you sell will be sacrificed at a special ceremony. Luxury craftsmen also buy slaves from you for sacrifice to their patron gods.

You lose again.

○ ○ ○ Uh-oh!

HOW TO LOSE YOUR HARD-EARNED STUFF

Before leaving home, turn your tortilla griddle upside down for luck. Once you reach the market, find three other *patolli* players. Get settled around the cross-shaped game mat, which is divided into 52 squares. When it's your turn, throw the "dice"—beans marked with different dot numbers. Move your colored stones the correct number of squares. As in Parcheesi, keep playing until you go all the way around the board. The first player back "home" wins. If you lose, and keep losing, you might lose all your possessions. It's not illegal to gamble, but to make your living that way is considered shameful. You may even end up gambling yourself away—into slavery.

CHAPTER 8

Temple Jobs

In a society that worshipped many gods and goddesses, each with his or her own temples and rituals, many Mesoamericans held religious jobs. Both nobles and commoners served as parish priests in small neighborhood temples, as teachers in *calmecacs*, and as officials in the major temples. In some groups, such as the Tarascans and the Maya, priests were allowed to marry, while in others they were not. All priests carried out numerous private and public rituals as part of their job. The Aztecs, for example, held 18 festivals a year (one for each month) that involved the ritual sacrifice of human beings. Other rituals called for the killing of animals and birds or the piercing of one's own flesh to draw blood.

High Priest

Sorcerer

As a senior Aztec priest, you probably made pilgrimages to the sacred city of Teotihuacan with the emperor. Your life of service and devotion obviously impressed him, because he has given you the title Quetzalcoatl. You share the highest-ranking religious job in the empire with another Quetzalcoatl priest. He heads the temple on top of the pyramid dedicated to the rain god Tlaloc, and you run the twin temple of the war god Huitzilopochtli.

People today would think you look very scary. Your face and body are painted black, and dried blood clings to your long, unwashed hair. Every night you pierce your earlobes, tongue, or other parts of your body with maguey thorns and offer the blood to the gods. Some of the blood from this daily autosacrifice, as well as the blood of sacrificial victims, ends up on you.

People of your time describe you as "a knower of the land of the dead, and knower of the heavens" and "wise in the arts of magic." Some say you are a priest of Nahualpilli, the god of magicians. Others see you as a healer. Some think that you work with the spirit world to bring rain to the earth. Still others say you can turn yourself into an animal at night and cast spells. (During the Spanish Conquest, the Aztec emperor Moctecuhzoma II sent sorcerers to cast spells on the invaders.) All in all, you're a bit of a mystery, wizard man. And much feared.

Priestess

Your parents may have chosen your career for you when you were a baby. After graduation from school, you enter the priesthood. When you're older, you may go back to your old temple school to teach. On festival days, you help with the ceremonies, sweep the sacred sites, and perhaps light the ritual fires. During the ceremony of the maize goddess, for example, you dress up like the goddess and parade with the other women priests through the streets, singing and tossing maize kernels and pumpkin seeds into the crowds to help ensure a good harvest. (The Aztecs always put on a good parade.) If a man asks you to marry him and you accept, he must get permission from the temple and your family before you can leave the priesthood.

THE BLOOD OF TREES

Throughout Mesoamerica, priests in their temples and people in their homes burned copal incense during rituals as an offering to the gods. They placed the sticky sap, or resin, of copal trees in "censers," long-handled ceramic incense burners that looked like frying pans. As the "blood" of trees, the resin was seen as a food for the gods. Turning it into sweet-smelling smoke was a way to serve it to them up in the heavens.

Teacher-Priest

You live in the *calmecac*, the school for noble boys. It is one of the more than 70 buildings inside the walls of Tenochtitlan's sacred zone. You teach the duties of a priest to those noble boys who will join the priesthood, as well as to promising commoner boys. The most important duty is performing rituals properly so that the gods will be pleased. These rituals include burning incense, keeping the sacred fires burning, and making offerings.

Student Priest

When you were a baby, your mother and father took you to the temple and asked the priests to educate you. After giving cloaks and food to the priests, your parents said a prayer and a small jewel was put into a cut made in your lower lip. Your pierced lip was a sign of the agreement made between the gods, the priests, and your family.

Between the ages of eight and fifteen, you begin boarding at the *calmecac*. In addition to your studies, you help sweep the school, cook the meals, make body paint from ashes for the priests, and carry wood for the fires. You'd better behave yourself. A common punishment was forcing naughty students to inhale the smoke of burning chili peppers.

I have pine boughs to decorate the temple.

I have maguey spikes for the temple offering.

I have firewood for the temple fires.

I have green canes to decorate the temple, too.

A good day's work, boys. Starwatching class next.

Day-Count Reader

After a baby is born, the parents visit you so that you can give their new son or daughter a calendar name. The naming ceremony of a child cannot take place without a day-count reader, or calendar priest (or priestess), as you are also called. You open your special book of day-signs and numbers (it is the only painted book that commoners regularly see). Some day-signs and numbers are lucky; others are the opposite. If a boy's birthday falls on Seven Deer, his future holds fame and success in war, but if it falls on Two Rabbit, he might drink too much and make a fool of himself. Fortunately, if a child's birthday falls on an unlucky day, you can read up to four days ahead for a better one. This system of connecting a person's birthday to his or her destiny resembles modern astrology.

"One Crocodile, Two Wind, Three House, Four Lizard, Five Serpent, Six Death, Seven Deer, Eight Rabbit, Nine Water, Ten Dog, Eleven Monkey, Twelve Grass, and Thirteen Reed — These various days, as it was said, all were good. He who was then born a nobleman, it was stated, would be a lord, a ruler; he would prosper; he would be rich and wealthy. And if a commoner were then born, he would be a brave warrior—a valiant chief, esteemed, honored, and great. He would always eat. And if a woman were then born, she would also prosper and be rich."
— *Florentine Codex*

Hmmm ... Maybe we should read ahead to find a luckier day.

CHAPTER 9

Ceremonial Jobs

Most large Mesoamerican communities had a public plaza where their citizens gathered for religious ceremonies. For people to continue receiving what the gods provided, the divine forces needed to be thanked. Even turkeys had a festival dedicated to them. Eggshells were sprinkled on the streets to thank the gods for this valuable source of food.

Performing properly on these occasions was very important. In Aztec society, both noble and commoner teenagers attended a "house of song." In these richly decorated buildings, boys and girls learned how to sing the religious songs, how to dance, and how to play musical instruments. Mesoamerican commoners couldn't read, so they learned about their society's world view through songs and religious festivals, much as early Christians learned the lessons of the New Testament through "Mystery" plays.

Did the Aztecs have any fun? At one ceremony, women healers and midwives threw balls of Spanish moss and marigolds at each other in a mock battle. That certainly sounds like fun. And although the ballgame had religious meaning, it also was played for sport.

Professional Ballplayer

Throughout Mesoamerica, the team sport you play was popular for more than 3,000 years. Today's historians have a simple name for it—"the ballgame." However, the Aztec version, *ulama*, could just as easily be called "bumball." In football, players kick the ball with their feet. *You* bounce the ball off your bum or hip as well as your arms. Be warned, though: The ball isn't a wimpy air-filled one. It's solid rubber and weighs 3 to 4 kg (6 to 8 pounds).

The game is played on a walled stone court shaped like a capital *i*. You and your teammates try to drive the ball into the other team's end zone by passing it to one another and bouncing it off the walls. You hope that one day you will manage to bounce the ball through one of the two stone hoops at center court. If this ever happens—it's very difficult to do—you will be a great hero and receive special gifts from the king after the game.

By your time, the ballgame is no longer the mainly religious event it once was. Nevertheless, the ball and its movement through the air still represent the battle between the sun and the moon, and between day and night. The opposing teams are still seen as acting out the struggle between opposites: for example, life and death or good and evil. And as in all ritual events, music, song, and dance play a major role.

Master of Cremation Ceremony

You have been summoned by the family of an Aztec commoner who has died. It is your job to make sure the dead person is sent off to the underworld properly. You wrap the body in cloth. Then you place paper "passports" on it to allow the person to pass through the regions of the other world safely. A jar of water is set beside the body so that the person doesn't get thirsty. You make sure that a sacrificed dog, the tools of the person's trade, and food are placed on the funerary pyre. During the cremation ceremony, you burn incense as priests sing a funeral poem. The ashes are placed in a clay vase and buried.

GATHERING TEARS

During the Aztec mourning period, the female relatives of the dead person didn't wash their hair or faces for 80 days. Special ministers then collected the tears and dust on the women's faces and wrapped them in paper. They took the pieces of paper to the temple and then to a sacred place outside the city. After the women had made offerings of copal incense, this time of great sorrow came to an end.

Volador

You're a Mesoamerican version of today's bungee jumper. In a New Year's ritual, you and three other "fliers" dressed as sacred birds climb a 30-m (100-foot) wooden pole to a platform. Another performer stands in the center of the platform to represent the sun. Four long ropes are wound around a cylinder above the platform. As musicians play below, you tie the end of one of the ropes around your ankles. Let's hope you're good at tying knots, because at a signal you and the other fliers dive headfirst off the platform.

As the ropes slowly unwind around the cylinder, you rotate 13 times around the pole. (Don't worry. The number 13 isn't unlucky; it stands for the 13 major gods and the 13 layers of the sky.)

The voladors' daring flights add up to 52 revolutions, the number of years in a calendar round, or cycle.

AHHHHHHHHH!

"He [King Motecuhzoma] singled out, by means of gifts, all the singers, the singers from the common folk, the song-writers, the composers, the beaters of drums—the ground drums, the two-toned drums; two-toned drum players, those who started the singing, those who led, those who gave the pitch, and those who whistled with their fingers."
— *Florentine Codex*

Drummer

In Mesoamerica, stringed instruments don't exist. You can, however, bang on a drum, shake a rattle, bong a wooden gong, or toot on a conch-shell trumpet or clay flute. Mesoamerican musicians don't play for an audience that listens quietly or squirms in their seats. Your group accompanies poet-singers, dancers, and voladors.

You play the most important instrument. No one can sing or dance until you are there to play your drum made from a hollowed log. Some modern researchers suggest that the rhythmic beat of a drum alters brainwave patterns and reduces stress. A group of people listening to a repeated drumbeat seem to experience a shared brainwave state. In your day, during some celebrations, it is seen as a bad omen if you throw off the beat by mistake—the event is canceled and everyone goes home.

Conch-Shell Player

You blow a conch shell on special occasions and also to wake up the city in the morning. It makes a sad, foghorn-like sound. All you need to do to turn a large conch into a trumpet is to get rid of the poor mollusk inside and drill finger holes in its former home. Priests may have used these trumpets to carry their prayers to the ears of the gods.

If you'd like a musical instrument with more notes, you can always learn how to play a clay flute. It usually has five notes. Just be sure you pick up the right flute before you head out the door to play at a festival honoring an important god. You don't want to be caught playing a flute made in the shape of one god if the festival is a celebration for another god.

SACRED SOUND

In a city today, most of what we hear is mechanical—the squeal of leaf blowers, the buzz of saws, the wail of sirens, even the ring of cellphones. But in ancient Mesoamerica, people's ears were tuned to the sounds of nature or to the rhythms of people sweeping, grinding, or hammering.

In Tenochtitlan, the loudest sound people heard may have been the deep beat of the giant drum at the top of the Great Temple. It could be heard 10 km (6 miles) away, its sound carrying across the waters of the lake. Even today, the magic of sound is used in religious ceremonies and to call people to worship. To hear what several Mesoamerican instruments sound like, you can visit the Princeton Art Museum website (www.princeton artmuseum.org/Jaguar/jaguar.html).

Matchmaker

Your job is to help young men and women get married. You're not a wedding planner, though. You try to convince a girl's parents that your client is an ideal match for their teenage daughter. Try saying, "He is a kind son," or "He has a good job," or "He has really long eyelashes." (Well, maybe not the last one.)

If the parents agree to the marriage, they send out wedding invitations. At sunset, after a big wedding feast, the bride is carried in a torch-light wedding procession to the groom's house. She wears earrings for the first time, special makeup, and new clothes. Once there, she sits on a mat beside the fire facing the bridegroom. You "tie the knot" by tying a corner of the bride's blouse to the groom's cape. Another feast takes place four days later with dancing, gift-giving, and solemn speeches by elders about the newlyweds' new duties as adults.

Dancer

With other young nobles and commoners, you learned how to dance in the house of song. You are now old enough to marry or become a priestess. This is the first time you have been allowed to dance publicly at the Toxcatl festival, one of the most important celebrations of the year. The fifth month of Toxcatl, May 4 to 23, comes at the end of the dry season. Food supplies from the fall's harvest are running low and everyone is praying for rain. As a reminder of the dryness of the season and the importance of rain in growing food, you wear popcorn-flower or toasted-maize garlands. You also wear red make-up on your cheeks, like the goddess of vegetation and flowers. Your parents would have a hissy fit if you wore it at any other time.

**"All day long we have made rain
In the courtyard of the temple.
With the little mist rattles we have
Called to the water in the paradise of Tlaloc."**
— excerpt from "Song of Tlaloc," *Florentine Codex*

Deity Impersonator

The ideal male candidate for the *ixiptla* job is described as "fair of face," "slender like a reed," and "well-built." Even if you think you could win a top model contest, you would not want this job. If the priests choose you, they will plunge a knife into your heart in the most sacred of all Aztec rituals.

Is there an upside to instant death on top of the pyramid-temple? In your world view, yes. Since you're a captive warrior, you would be sacrificed anyway. But once you have been chosen to impersonate the supreme lord Tezcatlipoca in the next year's Toxcatl ceremonies, you must train for an entire year. It isn't enough to look like a god; you must be able to act like one, too. You learn to play the flute and to speak and sing properly. It is a great honor to represent a god. You climb the steps of the temple with pride and dignity. It is said your soul will travel with the sun and be reborn as a hummingbird or butterfly.

THE NEW FIRE CEREMONY

Do you ever wish you could throw out all your old stuff and start again? Every 52 years the Aztecs did just that. They tossed out their old household pottery, figurines, hearthstones, clothing, baskets, and mats. According to myth, on this one day of the calendar cycle, the sun might not rise and the world would come to an end. All fires were put out and people waited in the dark for the priests' verdict on their fate.

The priests had two tasks during this ceremony. Their astronomers watched the night sky from a mountaintop. If the Pleiades stars made their trek across the sky as usual, the sun would rise and the world would be safe for another 52 years. But it would only be safe if the fire priests succeeded in their second task. They had to kindle a new fire on the chest of a sacrificial victim. If they succeeded, and they always did, the priests carried a flaming torch to a temple in the city. It was used to light hundreds of other torches. Messengers carried these throughout the city, lighting hearths in each *capulli*'s temples, schools, and private homes.

CHAPTER 10

Military Jobs

Every year, once farmers had harvested their crops and the dry season began, the Aztec emperor and his warrior priests led the army into battle. Some historians believe the Aztecs went to war to force other groups to send them food as tribute, so that they could feed the growing population of their island city of Tenochtitlan. Other scholars believe that the wealth and power of the *huey tlatoani* and his nobles depended on a constant flow of luxury goods and captive warriors for ritual sacrifice. Still others think both explanations are likely. Whatever the reason, warriors played a central role in the empire.

The well-trained Aztec warriors often won their battles, though the Tarascan army, with its bronze weapons, defended its borders successfully, as did some other peoples. The Aztecs never had to worry about an assault on their borders. Tenochtitlan was the largest city in the Basin of Mexico, and no other city had an army large enough to attack it.

Weapons Maker

Spy

You and your family make weapons or ammunition part-time. Your wife and daughters braid maguey-fiber slings, while you smooth rough stones into the round balls that are the slings' ammunition. If you are a carpenter, you may make dart-throwers (*atlatls*), bows, swords, clubs, or spears. As a stonecutter, you may produce sharp stone points for darts and arrows, as well as diamond-shaped spearheads and the deadly glasslike blades that are fitted into grooves along the edges of wooden swords.

You are a long-distance merchant. When the Aztec *tlatoani* decides to go to war, you disguise yourself as a local person and sneak into the enemy town. You hurry about, searching out bits and pieces of information in the local market that will help your king win the war. (Like today's newspapers, markets are sources of news and rumors.) No wonder spies are called *quimichtin*, or "mice."

You don't have any spy satellites or cameras to take photographs of the enemy town's streets or defenses. You can, however, draw a map. Military commanders will use your map to plan their attack. You are paid well in gifts and land for your dangerous work.

Eagle Elder

You belong to the most elite "knightly order," the Eagle Warriors. On special occasions, you proudly wear the insignia, or badges, you have earned for the captives you have taken and for your bravery in battle. You are too old to fight anymore, but you still play a part in military campaigns. You help organize the troops and have the sad task of telling women that their husbands or sons have died in battle.

"During combat they sing and dance and sometimes give the wildest shouts and whistles imaginable, especially when they know they have the advantage. Anyone facing them for the first time can be terrified by their screams and their ferocity."
— Spanish eyewitness description of Aztec warriors

Student Warrior

Welcome to "boot camp," Aztec style. Today's military schools may be strict, but the *telpochcalli* is rough, tough stuff. If you let your teachers down, you will be beaten or humiliated in public. Still, this is one way for a commoner like yourself to rise up the social pyramid. Great warriors are heroes, and you want to be just like them.

The Aztec army walks 16 to 32 km (10 to 20 miles) a day on their way to conquer a town. New soldiers carry weapons, heavy shields, ammunition, and food on their backs on these marches.

You can hardly wait until you have gone into battle and captured your first enemy warrior (usually with the help of an experienced soldier). It will mean the childish tuft of hair on the back of your head, which you have worn since the age of 10, will finally be shaved off. You don't intend to fail. If you do, girls can tease you in public at certain ceremonies, calling you a "big tuft of hair over the back of the head."

Jaguar Warrior

Your king has given you the title and uniform of the jaguar knight in a special ceremony. The jaguar is admired for its hunting skill throughout Mesoamerica. You wear your new uniform made of feathers with—GRRROWL—your head sticking out of what looks like the animal's open jaws. You have earned this great honor (only given to nobles) by taking four captives in a previous battle. The higher the rank of the enemy warriors you capture for sacrifice, the more rewards you are given and the more famous you become. Not surprisingly, two warriors sometimes disagree about who actually took an enemy soldier prisoner during a ferocious fight. The master of captives, a fellow jaguar warrior, listens to both sides and makes a decision.

Stone Slinger

Back home, you probably use a rope sling for hunting small birds and animals. If your favorite hunting weapon were a bow and arrow, you would be an archer. Both slings and bows are considered lower-class weapons because commoners use them. Throwing stones doesn't sound that difficult, but throwing them with a sling and hitting your target takes practice. An experienced slinger can fling a stone more than 180 m (600 feet) at high speeds.

Slingers and archers begin the battle by firing a deadly storm of stones and arrows at the enemy. You carry a heavy shield, but as a lowly slinger you don't wear the padded cotton armor and helmet of more experienced, higher-class warriors. As a result, you are more likely to be injured or killed in battle. With any luck, though, you will use up your ammunition within minutes and be able to move to the rear of the advancing troops, warriors who will fight the enemy in hand-to-hand combat.

Messenger

Do you like running relay races? If so, you should put yourself in the running for this part-time job. In times of war, messengers are stationed about 8 km (5 miles) apart along main roads. Passing information from one messenger to another is much faster than having one man run the whole route. The messages you carry from the emperor's palace tell allies when to prepare their armies for war. They also tell communities along the route to the targeted enemy town to have food ready for the Aztec warriors. After the enemy town is defeated and its main temples burned, messengers run towards home with the news of how many warriors were killed and how many captives taken.

HIGH-ENERGY SLIME BARS

If you get the munchies on the way to battle, you can always snack on a slime bar. The Aztecs used fine nets to collect a blue-green algae from the surface of their lakes. It was extremely high in protein and was made into small cakes and placed in the sun to dry. According to the Spaniards, these brownish bars tasted a bit like cheese.

CHAPTER 11

Health and Beauty Jobs

The Spanish explorers were amazed by the botanical and medical knowledge of the Mesoamericans. Today we talk about living a balanced life. The Mesoamericans were doing just that hundreds of years ago. They knew that a healthy mind and a healthy body went together. Female and male healers, who were trained by their parents, developed herbal treatments, sewed up wounds with hair, pulled rotten teeth, and set broken bones.

"What is it that you quickly take from its hole and throw on the ground? The mucus from your nose."
— *Aztec riddle*

Herbalist

You work in the Huaxtepec botanical gardens, in what is today the Mexican state of Morelos. Motecuhzoma I laid out these gardens in 1467, years before similar gardens appeared in Europe. Over many years of study, you have learned which medicinal herbs and flowers help sick and injured people. Your job in the large garden is to carry out medical research. Gardeners from other regions in Mesoamerica have brought strange plants to the garden and planted them there. Once the plants are growing well, you test them out on people who are sick. Even today, Nahuatl-speaking healers in central Mexico continue to use native plants and their ancestors' knowledge in their work.

Bonesetter

Midwife

> I've patched you up as best I can, but you mustn't run on those pyramid steps anymore!

You are proud to wear the turquoise earspool of the midwife. Like midwives everywhere, you help care for pregnant women and assist at the birth of their children. But in the Aztec culture, you have other duties as well. You play an important part in the dinners and rituals held before and after the birth. In fact, you should be prepared to give formal speeches on these occasions. In the two feasts held before the baby is born, family members make speeches asking you to take good care of the mother and child. You reply with a speech of your own, promising them that you will do your very best. The birth itself is a religious event, as are the bathing and naming rituals that follow.

If a patient comes to you with a broken arm, you put the arm in a splint to keep it still while the bone sets. Any injury affects both the body and the spirit, so you also say a ritual prayer over the break. If the bone doesn't heal properly, you perform an operation. You connect the two pieces of fractured bone with a "resinous stick." Today, this would be called an "intramedullary nail." The technique wasn't used in modern medicine until the 20th century.

GETTING SWEATY

The Spanish conquerors had never seen such clean people as the Mesoamericans. In Spain, it was considered unhealthy to take a bath. (The Queen of Aragon was proud of the fact that she had only bathed twice in her life!) By contrast, Mesoamericans cleaned their teeth, washed their clothes, and bathed every day. They also built small stone or adobe sweat houses. Ancient peoples around the world used sweat baths for both physical and spiritual cleansing. The steam helped sick people and new mothers feel better, and, like today's sauna, it was relaxing, too.

Barber

Your customers will not ask you to give them a very short haircut or to shave their heads. Those are not good looks in the Aztec Empire. Short hair is worn only by girls and boys under the age of 10. A bald head tells the world you're a criminal whose head has been shaved as punishment. Male commoners wear their hair a little below the chin with bangs, while warriors adopt the style of their rank. Generals, for example, wear theirs tied up in a sort of ponytail decorated with quetzal feathers. Like clothing, hairstyles show your place in society.

In your barbershop in the market, you wash your customers' hair, razor it into shape with an obsidian blade, and comb it. You also pluck out any facial hair with tweezers. This doesn't take long, because your customers have light beards.

Not too short, please!

Tooth Filer

Hold still now! I'm going to make you the best-looking young woman on your street.

You offer your customers the latest in fang fashion. "Face me and snarl like a dog," you tell your male and female clients before you start filing their front teeth with a narrow piece of stone. You have several different patterns to offer, from a T-shape to a point or a jagged edge. Young teenagers want their teeth filed too, but 15 is your cutoff age.

Mesoamericans also drilled holes in their front teeth and stuck bits of jade, turquoise, or obsidian in them. Archeologists have found some of these decorations still in place a thousand years later. You may be a skeleton, but your teeth will still be pretty.

CHAPTER 12

Beast, Bird, and Bug Jobs

A wide variety of wildlife lived in Postclassic Mesoamerica. These animals, birds, and insects were connected in various ways to the people's rich mythology and spiritual life, as well as being sources of food, dye, hides, bone, feathers, and shells. One in particular stands out. The now-endangered axolotl is a salamander, but unlike others of its species it never transforms itself from an aquatic larva into a land animal. It remains in the water and is magically able to grow a new leg if one is lost in an attack by a predator. *Axolotl*, the Nahuatl name for this small creature, means "water dog." In an Aztec myth, the god Xolotl tries to escape being sacrificed by throwing himself into a lake and is changed into an axolotl, a little animal with godlike powers.

Hunter

As a Maya hunter, you know the story of Hunahpu and Xbalanque, the Hero Twins. It appears in the *Popol Vuh,* your people's creation story. The brothers used long wooden tubes called blowguns to hunt ducks and other birds. During their adventures in the underworld, they used their magic powers to hide in their blowguns from a vampire bat.

When you were still quite young, your father or grandfather taught you how to blast clay "fowl balls" out of your blowgun to kill ducks in the dry winter months, when farming is not possible. The blowgun is probably your first hunting weapon. Using it requires you to creep up quietly on your prey and to aim well. These are skills you will need as an adult to hunt deer and other animals with a bow and arrow or a spear.

Dog Breeder

Your dogs will never win a ribbon at a dog show. However, they may appear on the menu at a ritual feast. The idea of eating hot dog seems yucky, but then again, some people today keep canaries as pets but eat chicken fingers. (Calling them "fingers" is a bit odd, too, when you think about it.)

The dog was the only domesticated animal in ancient Mesoamerica. When hunter-gatherers made their way to the Americas from Asia, they brought their dogs with them. During Postclassic times, dogs helped hunters track deer and other animals and were handy to have around the house. In the evening, they gobbled up any cockroaches that fell from the ceiling, warned their owners if a fox was about to snatch a turkey from its pen, and kept the children warm by snuggling under a blanket with them on cool winter nights. Like other ancient dog lovers, Mesoamericans believed that a dog would guide their soul in the afterlife.

As a dog breeder, though, you don't think of your hairless dogs as pets. You fatten them up on maize and then sell them in the famous dog market at Acolman in the Valley of Mexico.

"And the owner of a dog which had died put a cotton cord about its neck, stroked and caressed it with his hand, and said to it: 'Stand guard for me there! Thou shalt pass me over the place of the nine rivers.'"
— *Florentine Codex*

Tanner

You treat the skins of deer (*mazatl*) so that they can be cut into strips for painted books or made into sandals. Every part of the deer will be used. The meat is eaten, the bones become tools, and the hooves are made into rattles. Yours is a smelly job. After you've scraped the flesh and fur off, you soak the hide in a solution containing mushed-up excrement. The enzymes in the poo gobble up a layer of gluey tissue that would otherwise make the skin stiff once it dried. Another ancient way to tan a deer hide is to soak it in wood ash mixed with water, scrape off the flesh, and then put the hide in a solution containing the animal's own brain. The brain enzymes tan the deer's hide. Run, *mazatl*, run!

EATING BUGS AND SLUGS

People all over the world have always eaten bugs and slugs. The French and the Japanese, for example, enjoy land snails. The Aztecs ate honey-pot ants, fat white maguey worms, and jumil bugs as a source of protein. Today such foods are making a comeback in Mexico. Maguey worms appear on the menus of several fancy restaurants, and in Oaxaca and Morelos they serve up crispy grasshoppers cooked in chili oil. But these people know their bugs. You should not eat your neighborhood insects, because they could make you very sick. But you don't need to be told that, right?

Bug Farmer

Modern readers: Before you turn up your nose at raising bugs for a living, consider this. After the Spanish Conquest, insects called cochineals became Mexico's second most valuable export to the Old World. Only silver topped them. Even before the Spaniards arrived, the brilliant blood-red dye made from squashed cochineal bodies was traded all over Mesoamerica. It was used to dye feathers and cloth, to color food, to decorate books and pottery, and to treat wounds.

Cochineals belong to the scale family, those tiny, annoying bugs that munch through flower beds before gardeners even notice. Your "herd" lives on the juice of the nopal, or prickly pear, cactus on your farm in the southern Mexican highlands. Since the female can't fly, she defends herself against predators by producing a bad-tasting red acid. Pinch a cochineal between your fingers and out comes the dye.

The bigger cochineals that your ancestors bred from the wild variety are delicate creatures. They can be wiped out by a frost or a heavy rainfall. This is why you harvest your bugs before the rainy season begins and keep some pregnant females safe and dry in your house until the better weather returns. After you put the females back on the cacti, you have to stay on the look-out for worms, grubs, and ants, as well as for wild cochineals that will try to take over. Your own insects do best on young shoots, so you must also prune your cacti to encourage new growth.

At harvest time, you flick your cochineals into clay bowls with a brush or stick. This can take days and days, depending on the size of your cactus plantation. Then you spread the insects on mats and dry them in the sun. Unfortunately for you, they lose about a third of their weight as they dry out. To make about 0.5 kg (1 pound) of dye, you'll need 70,000 dried bugs.

Beekeeper

Your Maya ancestors first placed stingless honey bees from the tropical forest in hives they made, usually from hollow logs. They collected the honey to use as a sweetener and a sore-throat soother as well as an ingredient in an alcoholic drink made by fermenting honey and the bark of the balché tree.

Your beehive logs are piled in a small open-sided bee house with a thatched roof. You gather the honey a few times in the spring and once more in November or December. A special ceremony is held to ask permission from the gods to harvest the honey. It is an important trade item and helps to support your peasant family. You also sell the wax from the honeycombs to goldsmiths for use in their lost-wax process.

Fisher

You wade into the shallow waters of Lake Texcoco to collect the eggs that waterbugs have laid on the stems of reeds or on ropes that have been tossed into the water. You think the eggs are yummy made into fishy-tasting little balls and toasted in maize husks. You also collect tadpoles, which you like better than turkey, and tiny worms, which you find delicious cooked with salt and chili.

As a fisher, you of course catch fish, too. Fishers on the sea coast use weirs—woven branch barriers placed across estuaries—to trap shrimp and fish. They also build bonfires on the beach to attract fish at night. Both are new fishing methods invented in the Postclassic period.

"You who have chins, horns, and fins like beautiful featherwork or turquoise, come here and make haste to come for I seek you."
— *Aztec fisher's prayer*

Shell Diver

SHELL DUMPS

Although some shells were valuable trade items, coastal people threw away many more shells than they collected. Clams, mussels, and oysters were ancient Mesoamerican fast foods. You didn't need a special tool to catch them, and they could be eaten raw. After slurping down the soft animals inside, people crushed the shells to make lime or threw them away. Archeologists call these sometimes huge mounds of dumped shells *middens*. Studies of the layers of shells in a midden can reveal changes in an area's climate over time (different species live in different water temperatures) and show whether the shellfish were gathered by people who lived on the site or who just made a regular stop there in their travels (a shell's growth rings can indicate the season it was collected). Archeology has been called the science of rubbish. Now you know why.

If your skeleton is examined by future scientists, they may be able to tell what you did for a living by looking at what's left of your ears. Frequent shell diving from boats into deep, cold water can irritate the ear canal, causing bony growths to form. If you'd rather stay onshore, you can always collect shells along the beach. Two of the most valuable ones are the giant conch shell, used for trumpets, and *purpura pansa*, a shellfish that, when handled, squirts a fluid used as a very special purple dye.

The coral-colored Spondylus, or thorny oyster, is carved into high-class jewelry. In the early 1500s, the Aztec emperor Motecuhzoma II demanded 1,600 thorny oyster shells a year as tribute. That's a lot of these pretty shells to find clinging to rocks 6 to 18 m (20 to 60 feet) underwater. You and your fellow shell divers must be good at holding your breath.

Zookeeper

You work in King Nezahualcoyotl's zoo at Texcoco, one of the first zoos in the world. You care for animals, reptiles, and birds from all over Mesoamerica. Strange fish also swim about in pools fed by an aqueduct, which provides water for the lush gardens of the 300-room palace. If a creature is known to exist but a live example can't be found, it appears as a statue in the zoological gardens. Don't forget to polish those gold statues as you and your staff go about feeding turkeys to hungry jaguars, birds of prey, and snakes.

Aviary Keeper

From centuries before your time, Mesoamericans of different cultures used beautiful feathers to decorate capes, headdresses, fans, shields, and wall hangings. You work in the Aztec emperor's aviary, where exotic birds are raised for their feathers as well as for the enjoyment of the *huey tlatoani* and his family and guests. You and your workers feed the macaws, parrots, and other colorful birds, make sure they have water, and clean up after them.

The birds at the top of the aviary pecking order are, of course, the magnificent quetzals, which come all the way from what is now Guatemala. Their association with the god Quetzalcoatl make them the most valuable birds in the collection; you know that people have been put to death for killing one in the wild.

Don't bite my finger this time.

After the Spanish Conquest

The Spanish conquistadors took control of Mesoamerica's city-states one after the other, beginning in the early 1500s and ending with the fall of the last independent Maya kingdom in 1697. Even before the invaders arrived in a city-state, porters and merchants had carried contagious European diseases to the town or city, killing many and severely weakening the people's ability to defend their lands. Native healers simply couldn't cope with the deadly epidemics of measles, smallpox, and typhus.

The Spaniards settled the city-states with the best land or resources first, quickly changing the original inhabitants' way of life. The Meso-americans were forced to work for the colonists, adopt a new religion, learn a new language, and even wear new clothes (trousers rather than loincloths for men; sleeved rather than sleeveless blouses for women). Those who survived the epidemics and the forced labor found their world turned upside down. The conquerors introduced new tools (the wheel), new techniques (printing and glassmaking), and new animals (horses, pigs, and cows). Yet many ancient Mesoamerican jobs and traditions did survive, from weaving on backstrap looms to making tortillas to playing a version of the ballgame to practicing some of the old sacred rituals as part of their new Catholic faith. And although their ancient writing systems are no longer used, some native Mesoamericans today still speak the beautiful languages of their ancestors.

Tiahue intekitzintli means "Let's get to work" in Nahuatl. The Aztecs, Maya, and other peoples of ancient Mesoamerica must have said that a lot to each other as they produced their dazzling cities, artwork, poetry, music, textiles, and jewelry. Every year archeologists and other scholars uncover an exciting new find—a mural in a cave, a temple in the rainforest. Much remains to be discovered, but each little piece adds to our understanding of how these inventive people worked, created, played, and worshipped long ago.

RECOMMENDED FURTHER READING

Coulter, Laurie. *Secrets in Stone: All About Maya Hieroglyphs* (2001).

I first became interested in ancient Mesoamerica while researching this book. It's the fascinating story of how epigraphers—people who decipher ancient writing—unlocked the secret meanings of the Maya people's mysterious hieroglyphs.

Kimmel, Eric A. *The Two Mountains: An Aztec Legend* (2000).

In this retelling of an Aztec legend, the son of the sun god and the daughter of the moon goddess fall in love, lose their immortality, and are transformed into the two mountains overlooking the Valley of Mexico.

Lewis, Elizabeth. *Mexican Art & Culture* (2004).

As its title indicates, this book is an introduction to Mexican art and culture. Its chapters on architecture, sculpture, pottery, textiles, jewelry, masks, festivals, painting, paper, toys, and music link the traditions of the past with the lives of Mexicans today.

Mathews, Sally Schofer. *The Sad Night: The Story of an Aztec Victory and a Spanish Loss* (1994).

The Sad Night, which is illustrated in the style of an Aztec painted book, tells the story of the terrible last battle the Aztecs won against the Spaniards.

Menchù, Rigoberta. *The Honey Jar* (2002).

When she was a little girl, Maya activist and Nobel Peace Prize winner Rigoberta Menchù was enchanted by the ancient Maya stories her grandparents told her by the fire at night. Magical illustrations by Domi, a native Mexican artist, accompany this collection of tales.

Mexicolore Aztecs website: www.mexicolore.co.uk.

Click on the Aztec Pages link to visit a wonderful website on everything Aztec, from Aztec music and gods to stories and artifacts.

Montejo, Victor. *Popol Vuh: A Sacred Book of the Maya* (1999).

One of the oldest books in the Americas, the *Popol Vuh* is the creation story of the Maya. This retelling for young readers is beautifully illustrated by noted Nicaraguan illustrator Luis Garay.

ACKNOWLEDGMENTS

The work of many authors has made this book possible. In particular, I would like to acknowledge the work of Manuel Aguilar-Moreno, Arthur Anderson, Elizabeth Benson, Frances Berdan, David Carrasco, Sophie Coe, Charles E. Dibble, T.J. Knabb, Robert J. Sharer, and Michael E. Smith. Kenneth Hirth kindly answered my questions about stonecutting. A very special thank-you to Frances Berdan for her expert advice, patience, and kind words. Any errors are mine alone. Editor Barbara Pulling, designer Sheryl Shapiro, illustrator Martha Newbigging, copy editor Carolyn Kennedy, and the team at Annick Press have, as usual, done an amazing job. My thanks to Keith Urquhart and the Beaches Library staff for their help. I would also like to acknowledge the support of the Ontario Arts Council.

Index

Also look for these great books ...

*Cowboys and Coffin Makers:
One Hundred 19th-Century
Jobs You Might Have Feared
or Fancied*

**"Undeniably captivating ...
this informational gem
manages to stay fun and
entertaining while still
maintaining authority
on the subject. Highly
Recommended."**
—*CM Magazine*

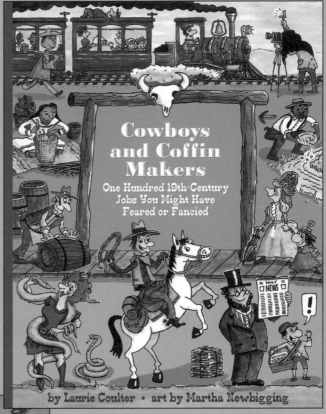

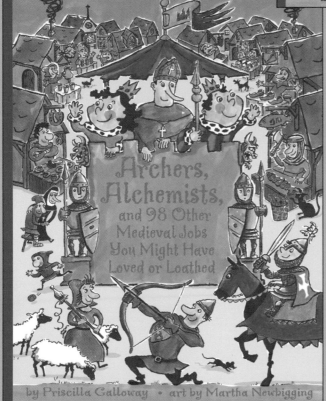

*Archers, Alchemists, and 98 Other
Medieval Jobs You Might Have
Loved or Loathed*

**"Witty, charming, and packed
with information."**
—*VOYA*